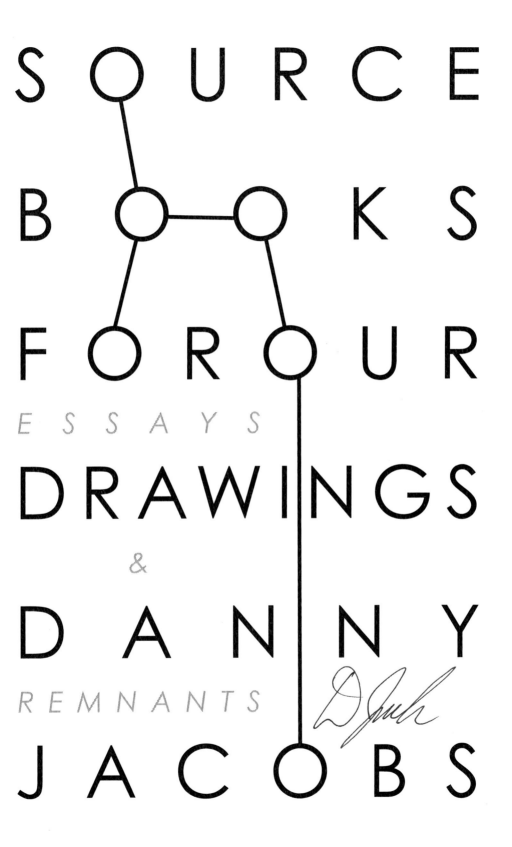

Copyright © 2019 Danny Jacobs

All rights reserved. No part of this work may be reproduced or used in any form, except brief passages in reviews, without prior written permission of the publisher.

Published with the generous assistance of Kathleen James in loving memory of Lovell and Vivian Lord

Cover design by Mark Laliberte
Book design by Jeremy Luke Hill
Set in Linux Libertine and Century Gothic
Printed on Mohawk Via Felt
Printed and bound by Arkay Design & Print

LIBRARY AND ARCHIVES CANADA CATALOGUING IN PUBLICATION

Title: Sourcebooks for our drawings : essays & remnants / Danny Jacobs.
Names: Jacobs, Danny, 1983- author.
    Identifiers: Canadiana (print) 20190085584 |
    Canadiana (ebook) 20190085592 | ISBN 9781928171805 (softcover) |
    ISBN 9781928171812 (PDF) | ISBN 9781928171850 (EPUB)
Classification: LCC PS8619.A254 S68 2019 | DDC C814/.6—dc23

Gordon Hill Press respectfully acknowledges the ancestral homelands of the Attawandaron, Anishinaabe, Haudenosaunee, and Metis Peoples, and recognizes that we are situated on Treaty 3 territory, the traditional territory of Mississaugas of the Credit First Nation.

Gordon Hill Press also recognizes and supports the diverse persons who make up its community, regardless of race, age, culture, ability, ethnicity, nationality, gender identity and expression, sexual orientation, marital status, religious affiliation, and socioeconomic status.

Gordon Hill Press
130 Dublin Street North
Guelph, Ontario, Canada
N1H 4N4
www.gordonhillpress.com

To the farm

CONTENTS

DIRECTIONS	1
ON HALLS, OR, AN ASHLAR FALLS TO THE CENTRE OF THE EARTH	7
ROOMS	25
COFFEE TABLE BOOKS	33
THE WEEKEND GOD: ALDEN NOWLAN AND THE POETRY WEEKEND FRAGMENTS	41
TINDERBOX: DISPATCHES FROM THE VILLAGE OF FIRE	53
GHOSTLY TRANSMISSIONS FROM JOHN D. ROCKEFELLER	73
TYMPANA	83
SHELF READING	93
A FIELD GUIDE TO NORTHEASTERN BONFIRES	97
THE BELLEISLE REMNANTS	121
Notes And Sources	133
Acknowledgements	137
About The Author	139

We should be able to find our way back again by the objects we dropped, like Hansel and Gretel in the forest, the objects reeling us back in time, undoing each loss, a road back from lost eyeglasses to lost toys and baby teeth. Instead, most of the objects form the secret constellations of our irrecoverable past, returning only in dreams where nothing but the dreamer is lost. They must still exist somewhere: pocket knives and plastic horses don't exactly compost, but who knows where they go in the great drifts of objects sifting through our world?

—Rebecca Solnit, "One-Story House"

With what shall I buy
From time's auctioneers
This old property
Before it disappears?

—Richard Murphy, "Auction"

DIRECTIONS

After Berry Mills and Moncton's slashed outskirts, upturned pine root in windrows; after the dump; after Maritime-Ontario's trucking complex, its field of hungry eighteen-wheelers and loading bays blinking in third-growth scrub; after the recycling plant's Matterhorn of glass, the emerald light of a million smashed Keith's; after the car auction, stumpwood cordage at the entrance; after Highway 1, the Big Stop; after Petitcodiac and the highway Mennonite church; after Anagance and Portage Vale; after Irving's tree farm phalanx, their billboards of clipboard employees and songbird conservation; after telephone towers high-stepping over clearcut hillocks; after the tilled fields of Sussex, its green-shade geometries and giant fibreglass cows, the metal blueberry man gone to Oxford; after the highway's corridor of stratified shale, pancaked and tagged, you take the Norton exit, the 124, its Liquor-convenience combo selling woodwork and camo hoodies; signs for Apohaqui; the riveted bridge crossing the Kennebecasis; the restaurant named Licensed Restaurant; *Me and the Mrs' Antiques*, bottle racks made from old rake-ends, stacks of Kennedy-era *Life* magazines and shelved Fiestaware; cross the four way at Evandale Junction, the Kubota dealership, clawed carapaces at rest; then you're on one more tilt-a-whirled stretch of rural New Brunswick, g-forced to your seat as you pass silo and trailer, Dad piloting the Taurus, the Grand Am, the Dodge Caravan, the Ford Explorer, your brother scowling into comics, your brother who almost doesn't come to the farm yet again, dropped off at the foot of Trites before the trip even begins, bitching since the morning, do we have to go again, I don't want to, never want to, fuck this shit, you can't make me; his weekend shot, house party and stolen booze a pipedream, and Dad almost caves, fine then, get out, you walk home; and your brother gets out, you're sure he does, his baggy pants windsocked to thin shins, booking it with fists crammed in his hoodie, fine, old man, I'm out of here; but somehow he is back in the car and we are tensely on our way; and you the carsick kid in the back, topped up with two tiny Gravol punched from their plastic sleeves, broken up, hidden in a scoop of Rocky Road, told not to look out the window, it makes it worse, focus on the floor, the lint caught in the fine nap under the seat, dropped dimes wedged in the raised fins of rain mats; but you look instead at birch cutting white against blue spruce and jackpine, birch bent from last winter's ice storm; past hydro poles and their dipping wires winging by in waves, keeping time with your rising gorge; past a taxonomy of barns; barns collapsed to rusted rooves like abraded skin, bow-backed in positive curvature, feline and arching toward the sun; or prefab barns, men on brand new ride-ons keeping a tidy lawn around the perimeter, industrial earmuffs cupped to heads, the blue-green of blown clippings fuzzing their shitkickers; your cousin rides the ride-on with the same calm attention, does the farm's back fields shirtless, his freckled skin proudly sunburnt, blistering and peeling in July to leave him white again, cutting the grass while the other kids traipse the property's back trails, as he bounces on the sprung pleather seat in the back half-acre, ten-years-old, hand resting of the ride-on's long-pole clutch; and you're ten too, one day younger, told to finish the Goosebumps once we get there, but there's just one more chapter, the kid can't remove the haunted mask, it's now his face, some ancient alchemy fusing it to his skin, and you get greener at the gills on the home stretch, shaky paragraphs as you curve past Peekaboo Corner, the Dickie Mountain Quarry, past Erb Settlement and Mercer Settlement; you're fifteen, you're twenty, and the route this far out has always been the same despite the new highway, a single solid yellow snaking out; past garbage bins built of two-by-fours and L-brackets, octagonal, garbage bins from repurposed chest freezers the only property markers; past Southern NB's unnamed logging roads, their ruts disappearing into the bush; past Midland Baptist where your grandparents rest side-by-side, the farm and their photos lasered on the black granite's mirrored surface and you wonder how long the image will last, a shallow haze in fifty years, unreadable like the oldest stones leaning at 45s against the pastureland; not at all like this foot-thick headstone worked to a doubled heart, its foundation stained aquamarine by corroded dimes—your family's superstition, a gift from Beyond left in shoes, on paths, the only thing to evade the broom after Sunday sweeping; and you remember how Nanny lived for five years while Grampie, predeceased, lay in the coffin we buried him in, grandchildren and sons taking turns with two spades after the funeral, one silvered at blade and scoop, engraved to Grampie for some ceremonial groundbreaking, taken off its framed mount for the burial; how at first it is ritual, funereal motion, a solemn handful of clay from each of us, yours with a rock that scrapes the coffin's spotless pine; how it builds up; how you have beers going now and you fill the grave slowly; how work gains its own momentum outside will or the body, even the urge to fill, the obligation; how the coffin's lacquered shine and grain fades, its curved lid like the hull of a capsized boat going under; how you think you find relief in the covering, the finality, just dirt on dirt, the work easier now; how the small group of uncles and cousins fill empty square-footage in shifts, resting like a road crew on break, one raised foot on the spade's shoulder, forearms crossed on the handle grip, hands dangling bottles; how the silver spade no longer shines, its polish gone matte with the scuff of stone and grave dirt; and afterwards Nanny smoking menthol slims and drinking cheap scotch like always, a bit of normalcy; still goes to Florida with her daughters, walks Sarasota beaches, missing him, still playing the host but the farm not the same so we meet up the road at aunt Wendy's while my dad gets wheezy from her cats; the farm inching ever downward, one more sagging structure in township New Brunswick, curled shingles, moss-fringed, cultivating its skin of ivy until you can remove the farm board by board, take out its skeleton of bent plumbing, take out everything that remains, that isn't portioned out to aunts and uncles, and the shape will stay, a net of limb and leaf, Virginia Creeper holding the shape of a vanished home; Nanny's death date still an uncut rectangle then, a raised ingot on veined stone, and if she ever thought of that blank—pictured the man coming down with his portable drill, worn leather case unravelling a sheaf of artist's chisels—you'll never know; and you're coming up on the Shell station now so veer right and downhill, feel your stomach drop before bottoming out to Belleisle Creek, its double-arched bridge, a glimpse of the barn's corrugated roof and the sunstruck water where every boulder worth its weight's above shallows, rocks you squat on after tubing and netting minnows, rocks you named as new territories, water reflecting black against the sun, stagnant, foam-licked, the spring freshet too many seasons away; and then it's there on the left, you've arrived, the one with the wrought-iron wagon wheel that's red-spoked, rust-blistered, full-caps curving the rim of it, scalloped edges from the acetylene cut: THE FARM, a name flouting its own cliché; hokey, that definite article, as if it's the only one footing these low Maritime hills.

ON HALLS,
OR, AN ASHLAR FALLS TO
THE CENTRE OF THE EARTH

Grampie got his hall for a song, a dollar, but paid a fortune to have it moved, shelling out for NB Power to cut the juice along the 124, have linemen down wire so a flatbed semi could truck it to the farm's property line, orange safety flags waving from its clapboard edges. A buck: no other bidders. Now I have to fill in the blanks here: Grampie's in a folding chair, the item list trifolded in his breast pocket, contoured to a pouch of pipe tobacco. He's out of his politician's three-piece, in his farm gear—faded Levi's and plaid gone monochrome at the elbows. There's a lot of empty seats, a few locals there to pick up repoed farm equipment, cut-rate acres in foreclosure. He's there for the hall and he isn't backing down. He has a few thousand in crisp hundreds, he has his chequebook, but hopes he won't need either. "First up. The former Belleisle Community Hall. Good bones. We'll start the bidding at one dollar. Do we have a dollar?" Grampie raises his little white paddle, what they always have at *Christie's*. "Good bones. Great bones. Solid maple interior. Sturdy stage. Turn her into a workshop." Grampie looks around. Shaking heads; downturned mouths. It's yours. Good luck moving it. I like the formal balance, the synchronous irony: he's in a hall, say, bidding on a hall.

Sold to the man in the back. He walks to the front to receive his deed, his rusted skeleton key.

*

I'm on break, on the library's front step, and the Freemasons are moving in these dog days of summer, the last remnants of Lodge 37 packed off to Sussex in pickups. Weeks before, I watched old men wrestle a mahogany throne—all padded velvet and gothic arch—down the stairs and out the door. Now Austin's standing over me, backlit by the sun, a squat negative asking for help with the ashlars, the hall's paired symbolic stones. Austin, proud Mason and building manager, says they're moving it all to Sussex, a bigger hall, a bigger town. The Masons are old hat in Petitcodiac, our riparian New Brunswick village. The public library lets the basement from the Fraternity, but for months the hall above us has been cleared of its mystic flotsam. No interest here. No promo, no Facebook. Petitcodiac follows a North American trend: masonic membership's been sliding since the 1950s, where it peaked at over 4 million in the US. Now it's down to a quarter of that, the lowest yet. The higher ups are desperate—there are calls for less secrecy, cuts to pomp and ritual length (Catholic-level). There's even suggestions to go easy on the formal wear, lose the aristocratic sheen, invite the kids.

When I was new as librarian, Austin asked me to join: "Young man like yourself, just starting out. Should be a Mason. It's not all secrets. And if you die, we have our own funeral. Take care of your wife." What would they do with my wife? Dark rituals? Sex Magick?

The Petitcodiac Masons sold cheese, though I want to say dealt cheese, such was the clandestine nature of transactions. Buyers met Austin upstairs in the hall; I never saw product change hands. Every few months the Amalgamated Dairies truck swung by to drop off another load. Was this community support? Where'd the cash go? Austin once gave me a brick of solid PEI mozzarella, one and a half kilos. I texted my wife a pic; it was the biggest piece of cheese I'd ever owned. Back home, I dug out the pizza stone and started grating: a two pie Friday night. I noticed while the oven was heating up: the cheese had expired months ago.

*

From *Heall*, the High German *halla*. Shares roots with *Hell*, the Germanic base for *cover, conceal*. Hell as a covered place, underground. Earliest definitions point to any place with a roof. Archaic European homes were halls, roomless: piled masses in sheepskins at the foot of the hearth, sleeping off their mead. One room. A roof.

*

Framed two-by-fours walled with tongue-and-groove knotty pine, leftovers from the basement reno: the clubhouse edges woods behind our house, a stretch of Acadian forest that goes all the way to Fundy National Park, crisscrossed with ski-doo trails and telephone towers. We catch frogs and salamanders along banks that hold the conical ends of beaver-gnawed birch on tamped-down mudbanks. The apostrophes of tadpoles make quotation marks with their shadows, and bolt at the approach of our rubber boots. The woods will be clearcut and developed shortly after we move in, the clubhouse dismantled. But for now, my dad is out there in 1990's July heat, hammer fall echoing through our new suburb.

It's my brother's domain, really—a hangout for his friends, a place where they read comics and trade baseball cards, where they stage the drama of exclusion that defines big brotherhood in the early grades, where they fiddle with his collection of *Spy Tech* toys—mirrored sunglasses, a fingerprinting kit, a camera disguised as a pack of Reese's

Peanut Butter Cups—cheap simulacra of petty crime and secrecy. I have only snippets of the clubhouse now—the warped narrowness like a country outhouse. Light through diagonal slats. A broken daddy-longlegs stuck in the whitewash. The clubhouse meant little to me, but my father's gesture in making it still interests me. Who asked for it? I know I didn't. Perhaps he thought we were lonely, my brother and I—about to start a new school, isolated in a new town's mid-summer doldrums. We needed our own place, we needed a hall. Maybe dad once had a clubhouse in 1960's Corner Brook, a place he squirreled off to after church, an oasis away from the crowded bungalow on Brookfield Avenue where he shared bunk-beds with eight brothers and sisters.

    I see him in our backyard, the age I am now—shirtless, arcing hammer, the clubhouse going up piecemeal after work and on weekends, sweat-and-curse stubbed-thumb Saturday mornings—and I feel a sense of obligation. The truth was I liked my room with its clean cloud-blue carpet, the lines from the vacuum still visible on the pile, smooth and rectilinear like a mown field. I couldn't play with my LEGO in the clubhouse. I was spoiled, but I like to think I had a sense of duty. I wanted to be good. I never stayed long.

*

Consider the childhood clubhouse or tree fort as miniature hall: its one-room simplicity straddling the private and the civic, the personal and public—groups selected for some arbitrary criteria, staging secret rites. Or a childhood fort as fort in the defensive, militaristic, sense—a redoubt against adulthood, reality, the wider world, a way to get back to the prelapsarian communal space, the original cave of the Dreaming Time. One room. A roof.

*

I leave the library's AC to follow Austin up to his empty hall. We're with another Brother—a quiet and scowly octogenarian named Sterling. I'm about to enter rarely trod ground, Petitcodiac's erstwhile sanctum sanctorum. In my five years of tending library below, I'd never gone up to the lodge. I'm the uninitiated, the awestruck laity, but it's a free pass today because ashlars need schlepping and I'm a picture of lumbar health.

The walls are lined with photos of past Brethren—white men in dark suits and gloves, sashed and tasselled, paragons of business when there was more business to be had in Petitcodiac; when people took the train up from Boston to stay at the Burlington, now torn down; when they had a shoe store, a millinery, a haberdashery; when they had a Chev dealership that sold wing-backed Impalas to the village upwardly mobile. All this unthinkable now, when so many go to town to crowd Moncton's two Wal-Marts, to pilot boxy carts at the Costco on the hill. There's a stage at the front, a middle altar of polished wood. The hall's carpet is a wall-to-wall cerulean, blue being important to the Masons (vault of heaven and all that); it's scuffed in places, its pile worn to grey. The air's trapped and textured; it carries the cooked dust smell of shut-up rooms, of attics and crawl spaces. It smells a bit of my Grampie's hall, decaying now in rural Kings County, less than an hour from here.

*

We use it as shorthand for hallway, yet hallways are the physical and conceptual opposite of the hall—one gets lost down hallways; hallways can be labyrinthine, full of doors to other rooms. Dead ends. Hallways direct us, give us directives. They're the thing we walk in nightmares. *Hall* suggests openness, a lack of division, all echo and space. You enter a hall through a hallway. The way to the hall. Perhaps we call hallways halls because we want to hang on to the word, to

Sourcebooks for Our Drawings

have halls in our hall-less, partitioned houses; to remove the walls, return to some earlier form of living. One room. A roof.

*

A strong memory from the compacted blear of the newborn months: I'm carrying our swaddled and sleeping daughter to her bassinet. I'm holding her in front of me like something sacred and easily breakable. In my slowness, in the care I take to learn each creaking floorboard, our hallway expands, becomes a temporary room.

*

An essay is more of a hallway. So what is this?

*

A giant letter G hangs from the ceiling, set marquee-style in green lights. The G's ornate, filigreed, maybe bronze. I wonder what it looks like at night, the G's bulbs burning, rapt faces lit with a swamp gas glow.

"What's it stand for?" I ask.

"God." Austin's eyes widen. "Also… geometry."

Or the Great Architect. Cadged symbology as floating signifier.

Austin brings up a dolly so I can wheel each ashlar to the stairs. It's one of those plastic scooters I haven't seen since grade school, the kind on casters from gym class, the kind we piloted on our knees, the kind that jammed fingers, a stack of them impaled on a wooden broomstick among the mesh bag of soccer balls in the storage room.

Every hall has two ashlars, a lithic yin and yang. The ashlars of Lodge 37 are light grey, about 10-inches to a side, cinder blocks given the totemic treatment, their faces carved in relief with the Masonic Square & Compass. I run my hand over the rough ashlar's unworked faces, symbolic of the Entered Apprentice, that Masonic fledgling. Newly quarried stone, flawed. If the rough ashlar is unenlightened man, then the perfect ashlar is Homo spiritus, the Master Mason, trued on all sides by study and civic good works. A leader among men. Austin nods to Sterling, "Like him." I heave them from their respective plinths, alarmed at the weight. Quick fears I've set in motion some *Raiders of the Lost Ark* domino effect—the idol removed, cogs and pulleys in the building's inner works springing the boobytraps that'll kill us in medieval ways. The ashlars are heavier than they look, as if all that allegory made them denser. I'm bent over the dolly, pushing each ashlar like a kid rolling his skateboard-prone little brother.

"They haven't moved since fifty-six," Sterling says. Fifty-six—the year they built this place, long before the library. The salad days of Freemasonry, rituals played to a packed house, the basement rocking with sock hops and village auctions, pancake dinners. The halls across North America not yet empty. One room. A roof. In their absence the ashlars will leave small squares of darker wood, untouched by dust or sunlight.

*

A hall is not a labyrinth. But I'm lost in the hall because its meaning eludes me.

*

My grandparents wanted a hall to extend their domain, expand the available square-footage in which to play host. They were connoisseurs of the shindig, the family gathering, grand architects of the 4:00 am hootenanny. Glazed ham perpetually in the oven. Haggard men popping in to take their beat-up guitars from fusty velvet cases. Fuzzy home videos of bottle-clink and din, faces of aunts materializing through the cigarette smoke, and the smoke-eater going for broke, huffing the collective tar-laced exhalations of 30 kith and kin. Grampie went up before midnight, snuck off, but I think he must've liked the noise below, proud of this amassing—half plan, half spontaneity—a product of his loins and hospitality. He drifted off to the stomping, the slurred guffaws.

If things had come off right, the hall might've been ground zero for these farm events, its scuffed hardwood taking the give of wobbly dancers and embarrassing dad-moves. Might've held our weddings, our wakes, our last hurrahs when the farm was on the decline. At the very least, it might've taken the runover when the old place got too crowded or the most sensible needed sleep. Hall as the after-party's open geometry. A place to see dawn with the stragglers, fishing the last warm beer from a cooler of melted ice.

*

I lift the rough ashlar, ask, "Am I the Chosen One?" They smile but my quip gets no laughs. They just want all this shit to Sussex, the ashlars moved safely without torn discs and traction. Halfway down the stairs, back arched, ashlar an uncomfortable pressure on my groin, I miss a step and almost drop it. "Jeee-sus. Careful, now, careful." Sterling looks nervous. "If that sucker fell on your foot." In extremis, the cheese comes to mind, a given block's own cuboid dimensionality, its ashlar-like heft. Each block stacked in the refrigerated dairy truck, staggered in flawless Vetruvian Opus isodomum. I bring the ashlar outside and half squat, half drop it into the back of Sterling's SUV, feel the suspension's give. What would it take for me to join? Honestly, I can't see a universe where I'd want to don the runic apron, sit through drawn-out Degree Ceremonies with these insular and exclusionary men. At the very least, I'd need more from this hall, more from the stone I just carried—a spot of magic crystallizing like quartz in its sedimentary heart.

*

My minor halls: halls of cub scout meetings where we stand at military attention, eyes front, the senior kids, the goodie-goods, checking our uniforms and grooming—the straightness of our sashes, the half-moons of schmutz in our nails. Always the same echo and dust. In high school, to Forester's Hall for punk shows in Moncton, *The Dead Fucks* putting baloney down their pants, spraying the pit with condiments, singing *Drugs are for fuckin' hippies.* As an adult I enter halls as the invited, reading poems in Mem Hall, the most hoity toity of my halls, UNB's mash-up of Georgian and Gothic, Milton's Eve and Satan in stained glass high above us. I tear Chase the Ace tickets at the Petitcodiac Legion—fundraising for the library—finding my groove in their main hall—two bucks each or ten for ten, the best deal. On stage buddy plays country covers and the seniors sip from Diet Coke and the boys from the village split pitchers, quitting time after laying asphalt in a heatwave week, and if your ticket's drawn from the spinning water cooler, and the cards are spread before you magician-style, everyone prays you don't draw the ace tonight; let it build all year, let the pot get fat, and let *them* be the one called up, their stub number echoing through the PA.

*

Grampie might've been a mason, and his hall might've once been masonic. Yet I remember no altar, no square and compass outside the door. More likely it had served the public for community functions, for bake sales and dances. Fiddlers up from Cape Breton, country bands on the local circuit, rough boys with their telecasters and sequined suits. Kids drinking stolen booze on hay bales. Fights out front, boys up from Sussex getting their asses handed to them by Belleisle locals. *Best get the fuck out of Hatfield Point.* These imagined scenes all take place in that spruce-lined corner of the farm's back field, as if the hall had always been there and not a half-kilometer up the road. And yet. Impossible that it could have been anywhere else except rotting into the ground on my grandparent's property. The way a building stakes its claim on eternity, on the subjective always-has and always-will. It seems so hard to move.

*

I keep going back to where I almost let the rough ashlar fall. I see it punch through the stairs in a rain of plywood, hitting the basement and shearing a square through the subfloor. It continues through cement, dirt, the layers of loam, clay, and bedrock, the ashlar ever falling, making a four-sided shaft miles deep, lines of perspective converging to a vanishing point as it falls through the mantle like a stone through water, gaining the density of a dwarf star, not stopping until it merges with the hot centre of earth's iron core.

*

Our many halls, our lost and decaying forts: rooms we try to fill, make echo.

*

After the ashlars Austin invites me back to raid Lodge 37's one glass-fronted bookcase. The books are newish, a disappointment—no occult esoterica in cramped uncial Latin, no *Corpus Hermeticum* bound in human skin. I spot a gigantic scuffed bible embossed with the Square and Compass, silk ribbon lolling like a collie's tongue between its gilt-edged pages. Austin says, "Not that one." I go light, grab *The Lost Keys of Freemasonry* by Manly P. Hall—a small hardback with a solid purple jacket, name and title in conservative serif. I judge the book by its cover, equate plainness with cabalistic authority, for I have no knowledge of masonic canon and assume a splashy front all but guarantees consumerist fluff, Dan Brown hokum. So I find Manly Hall in this cleared hall, one of the last things to go, while down the highway my Grampie's hall is still filled with so much.

*

My uncle Gil spills his Harley on a stretch of road just down from the farm, his bike nearly spotless after the fact, a small dent in the gas tank. If not for the white cross you'd pass it every time, a cottager's plot of manicured grass up to the gravel shoulder. Somewhere around here. As if you'd expect lopped trees, blowdown. No funeral; he wouldn't've wanted it. We gather at the Belleisle Community Centre to party. A new hall, and get this: it replaced the old one. All the family and all the leather, 400 bikers drinking foamy beer in plastic cups, standing in the same place the farm's old hall once stood before it made the trip down the road. The party would've been at the old hall, the farm's hall, had the hall turned out, had plans materialized—the urn on a foldout table by the raised stage.

*

Manly Palmer Hall is twenty-one when he writes *The Lost Keys of Freemasonry*. It's 1923. A theological wunderkind, he publishes his major work at twenty-seven. Commonly known as *The Secret Teachings of All Ages*, its full title hints at Hall's spiritualist ambitions: *An Encyclopedic Outline of Masonic, Hermetic, Qabbalistic and Rosicrucian Symbolical Philosophy: Being an Interpretation of the Secret Teachings concealed within the Rituals, Allegories and Mysteries of all Ages*. A Google search yields high cheekbones and furrowed brow, lampblack eyes staring us down through the cloudy scrim of 1920's portraiture. A vampiric cross between Valentino and Houdini, he looks like a villain from the silent era. A physiognomy that says *I know things*. I see all entrances accompanied with a flourish of cape, Hall leading seances in Jazz Age mansions while tailored men try to act brave and flapper girls fan themselves with their cloche hats. Hall in his filigreed grand halls, performing occult and arcane rites.

*

There are halls in the front rooms of old mansions, formal spaces where guests awaited the master of the house. Crossed muskets and a coat of arms. The farmhouse proper has no hall but my grandparents named the rooms—the blue room, the pine room, like some ancestral manor.

*

Beowulf's mead hall, *The Little House on the Prairie*'s one-room schoolhouse. Country churches, abandoned churches. The hall as universal stand-in, colouring my literary pyschogeography. There's a bit of the hall in every aging building I enter. College registrant's offices, used bookstores, underfunded school gyms. Echoic architecture. Motes sparking in the slantlight. That smell. Old paperbacks come close, old glue and cigarette smoke, or the stale sweet mildew on the cardboard sleeves of basement vinyl. One only need say hall and I hear our reverberating footsteps—my cousins and I entering from the farm's field, forcing the stuck double doors, blind from the sun, the hall still holding the last of the night's cool air.

*

Time is the differentiation of eternity devised by man to measure the passage of human events. On the spiritual planes of Nature it is the space or distance between the stages of spiritual growth and hence is not measurable by material means. Many a child comes into this world a Grand Master of the Masonic School, while many a revered and honored brother passes silently to rest without having gained admittance to its gate. The Master Mason is one whose life is full, pressed down and brimming over with the experience he has gained in his slow pilgrimage up the winding stairs. So saith Manly.

*

My friends and I build a fort in middle school—downed birch nailed to a triangle of three thick spruce. We are suburban kids and hardly handy. We cut down little; rather, we nail up felled logs from the deadfall. We don't much sit in our fort, for we fear its imminent collapse. We carve our names in damp woodflesh under bark. We talk about the girls we like, how we might get up their shirts. We hook our thumbs in our jeans and show each other new pubic hair. We compare. We lower ourselves into Red River's weave and rill and come out red and goosebumped. With our hatchets in our belt loops, our pants halfway down, we are brothers, or something even closer, more fleeting.

*

When Grampie got the farm in '78, he planted spruce saplings around the perimeter for a windbreak. He put the leftovers around the hall, and now they stand 30 feet, shadowing the white clapboard so it's half-hidden from the back field. Last summer I visited the farm but didn't have the key to the hall; I walked up through spider webs and overhang with my daughter strapped tight to me in her carrier, the ground spongy with fallen needles. I cupped my hands to the glass, smelling baked spruce gum. I tried to see past my own reflection. I tried to see the ghosts.

*

Manly Hall's *The Lost Keys of Freemasonry* is short, polemical, a fervid mix of Eastern philosophy, early Christian mysticism, and occult jargon, a text meant to reacquaint the Fraternity with its historico-cultural roots. Hall won't become a Mason until well into his fifties, but his Freemasonry is sacred, ancient, "its rituals ring with the words of enlightened seers and illuminated sages." He espouses a staunch anti-materialism throughout ("Matter is the tomb"). The Masonry of *The Lost Keys* is framed as spiritual quest, an attempt to lift the veil. For Hall, the true Mason is "capable of seeing through the blank wall and opening the window which is now concealed by the rubbish of materiality." The upright Apprentice is there for admission to the Mysteries; he trades hobnobbery for gnosis. What would Manly Hall think of Austin's hall, its parochialism and cheese racket, its gussied up men? Hall so young, so hungry for the *mysterium tremendum*. Did Manly have a fort as a child, a redoubt, a place he went to escape, to practice his fire sermons, the strange mystical boy of Peterborough, Ontario? What would Hall think of Grampie's decaying hall, its accumulated layers and carted-off detritus, that "rubbish of materiality"? A chance for something transcendent buried under three generations of boxes.

*

Every house has a drop site, the final stop before the yardsale. The embodiment of plans deferred. The raised stage of the farm's hall holds a coin-op pool table stacked with mildewed boxes; there's a few balls left—the old kind, each number outlined in a thick black ring. It must still be there—the balls unreadable through their accumulated dust, cue balls and ace approaching the same tarnished grey. And years later I feel the comfort of pool halls in cities, playing strangers with my own cue, for at some level I'm sure the crack of pool balls in an open room brings me back to the hall and its buried table–the bedrock of all that junk.

At one point the hall held the cedar walls of a sauna. I imagine Grampie dickering with a sunk hotelier, throwing the gutted wood in the back of his pickup, the igneous stone too, the kind you ladle with water to make more steam, bringing his load down the hill, pipe clenched in a shiteating grin. Those boards leaned against the back of the hall throughout my childhood, moldering plans of some Nordic pipedream.

Later still the hall held the furniture of extended family members when they were between apartments, between jobs, between lives, when they u-hauled their shit from the city to come back home, to go back to the folks for a bit, back to the hall, to curl oneself in the sheets of childhood beds. And I'm certain some of that stuff stayed, remained in moving's compartmentalized limbo, strata to be excavated in years to come.

*

The Lost Keys of Freemasonry is published by the Macoy Publishing & Masonic Supply Co., Inc. of Richmond, Virginia, an outfit still kicking. Robert Macoy, company founder, boasted a CV positively sopping in 'Grand's: "Past Grand Secretary and Deputy Grand Master of the Grand Lodge of New York and as Grand Recorder of the Grand Commandery of New York, and as founder of the Chapter system of the Order of the Eastern Star" (from the website's "About Us" section). Macoy spent some time in halls.

Macoy now stocks all manner of Masonic swag. In addition to what you'd expect (books, rings, sceptres), there's a Dollar Store's-worth of novelty scrap and costume minutiae. Under "Gifts & Novelties" I find the Masonic Beer Koozie, I find the Masonic Passport ("because Masons share a common citizenship which is not based on national boundaries... Not a Legal Passport"). There's the Masonic coaster ("Laminate top w/ cork backing"), the Masonic Stadium Cup. There's tons of ties (standard and bolo), there's birthday cards, pens. Scads of stuff, all plastered with the Square and Compass. The scale of Macoy Co.'s retail operation goes beyond the profane and gives off a whiff of targeted marketing, corporate trade shows.

In *The Lost Keys*, Manly Hall assures us that "Freemasonry is not a material thing" and gets cagey about accoutrement: "Watch fobs, lapel badges, and other insignia do not make Masons." Macoy's endless supply of merch would have us think otherwise. I search Macoy Co.

for ashlars; I need to know if I can Add To Cart a rough and perfect pair. Surely they'd ship like anything else. I click to enlarge my only result: the Perfect Ashlar Masonic Golf Shirt (contoured welt collar & cuffs. Double-needle bottom hem.). This is not the hall I want. It does not echo and has no smell at all.

*

My wife and I make a hall with our daughter by pulling her blankie over us. We laugh in the sunlight's dapple, everything tinged through the crochet. It's like light after rain, an atmospheric change. We're inches apart. We're its structure, the loadbearing walls—the only thing holding up this hall. One room. A roof.

*

An essential part of Masonic ritual involves circumambulation, a slow clockwise circling of the lodge. This silent walkabout is mimetic, the Masons following the motion of the sun, venerating their central altar like Druids rounding some chthonic cairn. It's winter now. On quiet nights in the library—no one in, the furnace off—I hear the building settle, a play of temperature and atmospheric pressure, tiny expansions and contractions moving like embolisms through wood, brick, and siding. It spooks me at my desk, that sourceless tick and pop. Sometimes it sounds like footsteps—our absent Freemasons circumambulating their empty hall above me. Heads down, spangled like Victorian dukes, they form their slow procession to nowhere.

*

Nanny and Grampie are gone and their hall will one day follow them—a controlled demolition, an excavator perched on a hill of wreckage like a crow on roadkill, jerking splintered boards into a waiting dump truck. If I had my way, if I had money, I'd move it again, hire men or move it myself, get her up on jack screws, adding box cribs like Jenga until it loomed above us, like ancient magic made it float. We'd back the flatbed underneath and take it on down the road, just like Grampie did. And God knows where I'm taking it, why I'm saving it, but it's forty years later and we're on the highway again, reckless drivers, running from the wrecking ball while curled shingles spiral in the wind.

ROOMS

> That handful in our skull might hold more distance
> than the lights from the edge where our telescopes
> shrug hopelessly and turn around for home.
>   — Albert Goldbarth, '"Far": An Etymology'

Chuck forgets we're pregnant. My father-in-law comes home from work and stares at his daughter's belly, tired, bewildered. Sarah's most disturbed by his face, that blankness. *You're pregnant*, he had said, over and over. *How far along?*

*

But forget seems wrong here, implies misplacement, possible recovery—an object half buried, obscured by silt but still showing outlines. Something one can dig up with effort, sustained will; come upon unexpectedly in that dusty room of lost things. To slip one's mind. Forgot my keys. Well go get them. Flip the couch cousins. What coat were you wearing?

*

My wife is six months, a perfect sphere taut against her dress, her belly button a stretched smoothness. It's Thursday night and she's there for Thursday Night Dinners, a weekly ritual that's earned its official name. A night when I work late, a night of familial updates, a night to share the news— of us, of work, the baby, what Sarah's measuring, how she's feeling. Talk of the baby room, the new Keekaboo change pad, pricy and curvilinear— non-toxic and low maintenance. This Thursday Night Dinner Chuck comes home heavy-footed, swinging his lunch can into the kitchen. A quiet man but quieter than usual. Later he'll say he didn't remember the drive home. He drops into his La-Z-Boy, looks at her belly, and doesn't know. After months of knowing, he doesn't.

*

After panicked questioning, after telecare, there's the ER, the CT, the MRI, the next few days acronymic. By now Chuck says he remembers, but we're grilling him, *Do you remember what you had for lunch?* I'm terrified things will vanish; that the baby, now regained, won't exist in the next moment. That she's only tenuous now, there by suggestion. That we're making her for him, but it's not really her.

*

It's not a brain tumor, technically, but a tumor of the meninges, the brain's protective layered sheath. It's benign but dangerous, an egg-sized mass at the midline of the anterior cranial fossa, the front part of the skull's floor, ridged and duned like desert aerial shots. When a meningioma starts to grow, doming out from the dura and faced with the cranium's rigid curve of bone, the brain gets compressed, displaced—a palm into dough.

*

A pressure, then. One fleshy object against another. Venous oblongs jockeying for space. The mind translates this into a cognitive void, a negative: our daughter growing inside his daughter. All those details and their contingent tendrils, carefully excised. What were the dimensions of his forgetting? How big was the room? Could you find its definitive edges? Plumb the layers?

*

Maybe Chuck's forgetting was a fade, the contours of memory dissolving in some cerebral emulsion. Or otherwise a short circuit: neurons tightly pressed by the tumor until they touched, the connections going all at once. A darkened room.

*

Four months of news: where does it go? The announcement on Father's Day—our daughter inhering in his mind from then on, our daughter that day newt-like, all vein, blurred blue organ and shadowy transfer under translucent skin, hiccupping and kicking, small nubs for ears, fingers almost fin. There's a debunked theory that says mammalian fetal development mirrors evolutionary change—at month two, in June, she was a small tetrapod on the banks of the Carboniferous. Ontogeny, day-by-day, recapitulating phylogeny. Geologic time telescoped to nine months. A ball of cells floating in the body's colloidal river. Chuck's cells dividing, too, but slower.

*

The meningioma is right of the falx, the part of the dura that dips into the brain's fissured middle. Falx: another name for scythe, its curved blade riding the length of the brain's two hemispheres. A symbol of our mortality couched in the Sagittal plane.

*

There's degrees here, percentages. So we're handed ninety-five percent and hang on, speak it to relatives, text this number back and forth. Probability as mantra. When hope ratchets itself up to math. Likely he'll be fine. It's close to the optic nerve, so when they go in, there's potential blindness. There's that. With the head and its dense ivy of nerve, you're always millimetres away from something crucial, some nest of essential self eradicated in the scalpel's slip.

*

I find a clinical representation of the meninges in a Google image search, three layers delineated in rolled-back cross-section—Dura mater, Arachnoid mater, Pia mater, each with their own pastel shade. All stratified things look the same in diagram: schematic, planar. Limned. They're featureless slabs, successive, lost in the white non-space of a textbook's glossy page. The mess of blood and fat, or stone, or current; all crack and fissure, blurred boundary, all that time, the entropic flux of the real, removed or contained. Deprived of its labels and the markers of scale, this googled image might be the Earth's upper mantel, a close-up of the skin's dermal strata, some field's upturned sedimentary rock face. It could be the sky's many spheres.

*

I can sit with lingo's distancing lull, rattle off the facts. Dura mater, *Stone mother*, the brain's tough outer covering, its leathery shell. The Arachnoid mater has web-like fibres extending downwards toward the brain; meningiomas are made of arachnoid cells and balloon from that middle layer. The Pia mater is thinnest and innermost, the only meningeal layer to follow the brain's infolding contours, cradling it. *Tender mother*.

*

Harder to picture the operation's gristle and glisten, its bone dust and suction, that slick palette of red, grey, and yellow white. Harder to think about what's at stake.

*

A week after his forgetting, Chuck undergoes a bi-frontal craniotomy, his half-shaved head steadied in the taloned prongs of a Mayfield clamp. When the surgical team pulls his forehead down, the frontal cutaneous flap makes a blood-and-tissue facemask. They drill burr holes to remove a bone flap of forehead—a rectangle framing the brain's two hemispheres. After retracting the frontal lobes, they use the Cavitron Ultrasonic Surgical Aspirator (CUSA) to empty the tumor. The name sounds fake, ray-gunnish, carries the golden age zing of sci-fi paperbacks. The CUSA hollows out with high frequency, its vibrating stylus boiling the meningioma's cellular gunk—it's a phase change through pressure reduction, not heat. After the tumor's fibrous insides are broken down and aspirated, its husk is collapsed and removed.

*

Mayfield clamp, CUSA, the high-density plates and screws that line his skull: Chuck would appreciate the tools that work on him, for him— neurosurgery's space age tackle. Chuck, the consummate handyman and perfectionist, a measure-twice-cut-once exemplar, a firm believer in a good tool. For years now he's shown me tools he got for a song at yard sales— vintage stuff with wooden handles gone black with grease and sweat. During odd jobs, Chuck likes it when a rarely used tool unexpectedly demands its use, the only tool perfect for this one moment, this nook or crevice. *Might have something for that.* He torques or ratchets, cuts or levels off, gets shit done, the tool's narrow borders of utility widened, all the while relating the story—*found this one on the side of the road a few years back. Just lying there. Good tool. Never know when you'll need it.*

*

The CUSA's titanium proboscis vibrates at 23,000 Hz along its longitudinal axis. Shockwaves in the tumor's shell. The moment of its collapse—crushed paper bag? Wilted rose?

*

The family waiting room contains its own smaller room, an anteroom for the direst cases. A door you can close. The elderly volunteer is gracious: *feel free, go right in, you can have some privacy.* Her green coat and concerned smile. I feel like we qualify for the room, our faces proof enough for access to its small perimeter. Better to be among the regular, the routine. People outside might have it worse than us, and I wish to forsake the room, pass it off to them. Give them this sad stab at domesticity—plastic plants, floral wallpaper, carpets a bad evergreen. Calming landscapes. The bland décor of chain hotels and nineties living rooms. Sighs of relief and garbled Thank Gods stuck in the walls, crumbled shock and wails of denial. Sanctum of anxious small talk. Square-footage defined by expectancy. A place of twisted tissues, distracted reading, a ten-foot-square distillation of what hospital seating really is— a place to wait. To await: news, results, the sliding doors and the purposeful well-groomed holding charts. And never has waiting felt so acute, every word and movement coloured with it, drawn-out time tangible, a geometry embodied in this small space. Sarah is terrified, crying and cramped, and we wonder about the stress on the baby. How much angst does this six-month foetus sense through some complicated amniotic exchange? I'm trying to read, scan Twitter, but there's the outer waiting room's door, the bright hallway beyond. Every ten minutes or so we go out to check for answers, will something to happen. The nice volunteer smiles and dutifully dials up—up to the powers that be, up to that amorphous place where there's answers, where Chuck lies unconscious and opened up in a white gown; a place where all is pale, bland greens and blues, except for one small daub of vital red crowded with focused people. The nice volunteer tells us again that there's still no news, tells us *soon*. We're trapped in the day's one long *soon*. I wander the wide and hand-railed labyrinth, beige halls of steel laundry carts and signage. Who knows where Chuck is now? In a few months, our daughter will be born on the second floor.

*

When Dr. Fawaz enters our small room—because it's our room now, we've put in our time—he tells us they got it all. He makes a dome of his steady hands, brings his fingers in—how they collapsed the tumor. There's reassuring terminology, next steps, but I don't hear much. Our thank yous are profuse, unselfconscious. We cry and hug; we are wild and red-eyed and reverent, my mother-in-law holding Dr. Fawaz's hand in both of hers. Routine for this serious man, a five hour stint before lunch. A day at the office. He's still in his scrubs, Crocs on his feet—that honeycombed sponge of a shoe all surgeons seem to wear. They're practical, no doubt, easily-cleaned; but they always look misplaced in hospitals— a shoe for toddlers and gardening retirees. There's blood on the left foot, a single drop, vermillion gone russet against the Croc's green. A welcome hint of medieval sloppiness. A coin of intimacy: it comes from a place no one else will ever see.

*

The weekend before the operation I built on a structure that Chuck started in my unfinished basement, a pine frame for firewood. Months ago he came with his canvas bag of tools while I was at work, his trunk full with scrap and level. He hammered together a few lengths of two-by-two to make a skeletal box that held birch, a neatly piled cord against garbage bags and the season's empties. I spent the morning attaching a second box to stack the wood two deep, drilling eight-foot boards to the ceiling supports while Chuck lay at home full of pre-op meds, the blinds drawn, sunlight painful now, any light painful, Kleenex stuffed into the sunglasses he wears inside. This slipshod construction was the first I did without him or his tools. I piled the box with birch, quartered ends stacked eye-level. It held.

*

All bilateral creatures form from three germ layers, a primal shelled ball. As the embryo grows, the endoderm develops into organs; the mesoderm into bone and skin. The ectoderm—the outer layer—becomes, among other things, the brain. All these with their own depths and lamina. All of us layers within layers, tripartite. Flush-fit nesting dolls. Orreries.

*

I want to see Chuck's procedure like this: when the tumor is removed—carefully brought out from darkness and into the UFO lights of the operating theatre, collapsed in its steel pan—the neural network that built our daughter in his mind, that was always there, starts to reconstruct her, its billion nodes, knitting back together what he knew of her; ultrasound printouts in their successive chains like photobooth clippings, unspooling through pain and morphine fog, coming back to him in high-contrast black-and-white—the blurred arc of her spine, a small foot in the dark, the heart a pin-hole aperture in the snow-static of her chest. Her prenatal heartbeat not like galloping horses like they say, not at all, but like some thin metal continually bent, a spacey wobble. As Chuck wakes up, her own brain is upping its regimen of cortical folding, gyri and sulci deepening into wrinkles. To hold more within the fist-sized dome of her skull.

COFFEE TABLE BOOKS

The family coffee table had a glass surface. My chore was Windexing both sides of its two beveled panes, scrubbing at hand smears and the opaque blue-white of coagulated spilt milk. A few times a month my mom took the glass out to get at the crumbs, pencil shavings, and tiny pink slugs of rolled easer that fell between the cracks where the panes, not quite flush, met the wood. Its stain was late-seventies brown, the dark walnut of yard sales and thrift stores. It was where my brother Jesse and I spent our childhoods drawing.

*

Our medium was dot-matrix paper, low bond, brought home in large boxes from Dad's work. I wonder if he asked the boss, or just nabbed them from the supply room—theft in the name of Art. A box lasted. I seem to remember one holding out through most of elementary school, although I'm surely conflating boxes, thousands of sheets attached end to end like uncut books, you'd yank the top sheet and they'd come accordioning out, a morning's worth of sketches in one pull.

Part of the ritual: carefully removing the paper's perforated strips, thin hole-punched pieces made to thread the printer's feed sprockets. Pull too hard, pull too slow, pull with too much angle, pull without refolding, and your paper rips raggedly down the side and you have to junk it.

Sometimes the paper was used, one side filled with old memos or expense reports, reams of triple-columned numbers. We favoured the pristine sheets, but we made do, sucked it up, happy for the paper, for the one blank side. But the printed sheets always bothered me, and I'd resent that dark shadow showing through from the other side.

*

The coffee table's six legs supported a lower level, a woven rattan that held our reference material—haphazardly stacked volumes of *The New Book of Knowledge* bound in faux-leather. My dad bought the encyclopaedias from a door-to-door salesman shortly after my brother was born, and they took prominence on the bookshelves of our childhood homes, their gilt spines giving our musty basement libraries a collegiate air. They were well-used in those pre-Internet days, splayed out on family room carpets and carted upstairs when we needed sourcebooks for our drawings, our skinny arms fully extended as we held their stacked weight.

*

Some letters of *The New Book of Knowledge* were better than others. The thick "A"—which included the entry for ANIMALS—was a mainstay under the coffee table, with its multipage spread of our geologic era's most fierce megafauna. I was fascinated with a black-and-white photo of a horn-rimmed scientist standing beside the mounted exoskeleton of *Macrocheira kaempferi*, the Japanese Spider Crab, its legs reaching a foot taller than the man. Behold, the Nightmare Creatures of the Deep! An early lesson in proportion.

*

Jesse and I fought as kids, at times viciously. One morning he threw the sawed-off end of a two-by-four at my face to split my lip wide open before school. He was a smirky kid with a smart mouth, the bane of teachers, and he knew how to get to me—small jibes I was too sensitive to ignore. Dad brought home the paper less for fostering creativity than for maintaining peace and quiet—probably the same reason they splurged for the little cushioned lap desks when we road-tripped to my grandparents' Florida trailer.

    These devices were no more than styrofoam-stuffed pillows topped with a kind of pressboard slate, over-priced at Toys "R" Us. Sardined in our sedan's back seat, we drew for most of the three-day drive down the eastern seaboard, filling the back seat with scribbled paper, my dad pulling over at rest stops every few hours so we could burn off the pent-up kid energy crackling in our limbs. Stuck in Bronx traffic, I grew whiny, asked to stop and look for the Ninja Turtles. Without those pillow-boards we would've gone feral somewhere around the Virginia state line, kicking each other unconscious and clawing at the upholstery.

    But we didn't fight at the coffee table. There's my folks clinking brunch Caesars on Saturday mornings, a few snatched placid hours while my brother and I doodled in the dark, in the dim light of *Duck Tales* and *Captain Planet*, the blinds closed to the day, our knees drawn up into our pajama shirts, our elbows almost touching, but not quite.

*

The encyclopedias had structural uses, too—large slabs for our action figures' secret headquarters, buildings that fell and crushed them. They had a solidity that outlasted the cheap goods we got every year for Christmas and birthdays.

    Colour photos were often blurry, dark, printed out of register like old 3D comic strips. Diagrammatic sketches came dispersed among entries, done in the monochrome blue of mid-century high school textbooks—an electron's bright blue ellipse ringing the black-and-white nucleus of a hydrogen atom.

*

I did rip-offs of the morning TV we binged on. Instead of my beloved Ninja Turtles, I did ninja frogs who fought with elaborate swords and clubs, weapons that smashed little two-legged robots, said robots almost exact copies of the Mousers, the robot minions of Baxter Stockman, evil scientist and Master Shredder's milquetoast lackey. I was quite pleased with the dynamism of these compositions, blind to their unoriginality—I smiled with my tongue out in concentration, as my ninja frogs, ever swinging, saved the universe, leaving behind them a junk pile of exploded circuitry and bifurcated robot hull.

Meanwhile my brother was creating good work, competent stuff that my parents and I marveled over. Even then it was comics—paneled strangenesses he does for a living now. His recurring character was Melvin, a Bart Simpson/Dennis the Menace amalgam who had X's for eyes, overall shorts, and a propellered beanie cap. Melvin was a brat and a joker, a shit-disturber, a cartoon extension of boyhood Jesse. The comics were crass, funny, and violent, the fumblings of a mouthy and imaginative fourth-grader enamoured with Pee-Wee Herman and Ren and Stimpy. The work was careful—preliminary pencil drawings erased, then inked. There were less-popular projects, too; spinoff issues barely started about minor characters—Melvin's relatives, a bumbling meathead superhero called Fartman.

I'd lose interest in my drawings after an hour or two. It was momentary stuff. I was undisciplined. I had no process. My grade-school attention span maxed, I'd bust out the LEGO and destroy the room while my brother continued on through the morning. I'd run round him, try to look over his head.

*

The encyclopaedias still stand complete on a bookcase in my parent's basement, a shelf of Oxford blue among Danielle Steel paperbacks and my grandfather's sci-fi hardcovers—old Asimov, New Wave anthologies with psychedelic covers, a Book Club first edition of Dune. When I'm over to borrow the leaf-blower, I filch "A" on my way out. They won't know it's gone.

*

In further artistic solidarity, my dad made photocopies of Jesse's comics at his work after hours. They were stapled affairs, folded 8½-by-11s, the standard size of all childhood ephemera—homemade cards, coupon books. A new release from J-Comics was a big event. I anxiously awaited the Melvin Christmas Special, the first full-colour edition, a one-off. Jesse worked on it throughout December and it was ready for Christmas. Melvin loses his shit and hilarity ensues. There was a decapitated reindeer in there somewhere, I'm sure of it.

This Christmas, with my brother home from Ontario, we brought up a box of our old work. Among report cards and ratty campfire notebooks, a stack of J-Comics. My parents kept them all. Most were unfinished, the last pages blank, their staples leaking a small penumbra of rust into their brittle spines.

*

I'm holding a volume of *The New Book of Knowledge* right now, the cover embossed with its gold-leaved tree, the facts therein growing more outdated by the minute, the datasets uselessly static, its physicality hopelessly impractical.

The boards are solid, the binding tight. Almost mint. They're built to last, but no one wants them. They're freight you lug from house to house, weeded at the library, denied at the church book sale, at Value Village. Value Village says no way, dump them, box them up, the thrift stores are swamped, load them on a barge to nowhere. A 15,000-page burden. Grolier's team of well-meaning teachers and gentle authorities are unneeded, defeated by Web 2.0's hive mind, their bound efforts *liber non grata*. The Anthropocene will define itself with a stratum of pulped reference matter.

*

My parents no longer have the coffee table. Jesse huffed it around Halifax in his early twenties, U-Hauling it from one shitty North End apartment to another. I suppose he drew at it well into his adulthood. I asked him but he couldn't trace its end. *I wish I had a cool story about someone falling through the glass*, he texts me. What became of it? Was it taken away on spring cleaning? Tossed in an apartment lot's Fero bin? Does it sit in some living room still?

Maybe its top was indeed smashed along the way. Without panes, it looked naked, skeletal. The glassed transparency gave it depth, the way it reflected the morning sun and stretched the light of our Saturday morning cartoons.

I have my own house now, with an antique coffee table my wife got at a downtown boutique. This new one is all barn board and weathered paint, a centrepiece. If the old table came back to me, I'd turn it down.

*

I read entries from volume "A" at random. The style is that anti-style of encyclopedias, the *lingua franca* of sleepy classroom filmstrips and Bristol board science projects. Some sentences are so general they're meaningless:

> *There are many reasons for the existence of archaeology.*
> *Languages may seem very different.*
> *We are used to the idea that we will age.*

*

When Jesse and I sat at our paper, we had to be careful to stay within the confines of our respective coffee table panes; too often we'd snap our leads when the pencil fell into a crevice where the pane rested, the drawing torn along the line. On newly polished glass, our work floated above us.

*

There's this impossible painting under AGING called "Life Spans of Animals," a juxtaposed arrangement meant to illustrate scale. It's a cross-section of sky, land, and sea populated with creatures in profile, their ages below each, always that white human male among them. The Indian Elephant beside the Horse, the Rabbit beside the Lion, and above them all, the Horseshoe Bat in flight with the Condor. Marion's Tortoise lives to 152 years, while the Giant Clam's age is unknown. I would've loved this page as a kid. I love it now. They'll always be there—mid-flight, mid-step, one foot ever so slightly raised, as if about to walk away.

THE WEEKEND GOD: ALDEN NOWLAN AND THE POETRY WEEKEND FRAGMENTS

> I've worshipped him myself, climbed the days of the week
> like a ladder, with every rung bringing me closer;
> and if when I got there it was never
> quite as good as I had hoped,
> afterwards it always seemed to have been better.
>
> — Alden Nowlan, "The Weekend God"

Nanny says Nowlan *lumbered*. She calls on Christmas, the year after Grampie died, and I tell her I got the *Selected*. It's one of my first poetry books, the one from Anansi, the one with the bland blue-grey fish house. For this Maritime Poet, the cover demands a bland fish house. "He was a big man," Nanny says. "Your Grampie and I would see him lumbering across campus when we visited for functions." Grampie – respected alum, federal minister, his honorary doctorate's black floppy hat hanging on my office wall, flattened and mounted under glass, *Hon. Gerald S. Merrithew, Doctor of Laws, Honoris Causa* sewn on a square of satin. Grampie, MLA for East Saint John during the Hatfield era and reciter of doggerel verse, might've known Nowlan well, might've known his poems, yet he doesn't have his books among his military histories and outdoor guides at the family farm.

After he dies, I find a 19th-Century Wordsworth with gilt-edged pages and tooled leather cover, the publication page missing. Mountain etchings for *The Prelude.* The last time I see him he's lying on a chaise lounge in the kitchen; he's wrapped in a blanket and it's the first time I've seen him unshaven. He asks about my poetry, asks if I've read T. S Eliot. I wish I'd asked him what he knew about Alden.

Nowlan *lumbered.* Can only the large lumber? I like to think it's the geography of UNB, the hill tuning our gait, nothing to do with size, the hill canting us, feet ahead, steps larger and longer, a lope, a saunter, the slow dip of the Saint John River Valley creating in our bodies a downhill compensation. Nowlan lumbering down Windsor Street—his big beard and big hair catching the snow, his tie blowing out behind him, his post-op neck distended as if he's swallowing the day's weather, his myth trailing behind his gait.

*

And we, too, lumber years later. To his repurposed home—Windsor Castle turned grad house, the downstairs full of formica tables, the upstairs offices where we get our student IDs, file our grievances. Which room was the bedroom? Where he slept, snored off the whiskey? There are framed copies of his best-known poems throughout. "An Exchange of Gifts" is installed by the front entrance: "I will keep on / writing this poem for you / even after I'm dead." And I want this to be true when I walk in after the angst-ridden one-upmanship of seminars, after I leave half in the bag, head down into a snowstorm, the door banging behind me.

See, we can't help but think this way. The myth grows, lumbers. And we grad students lumber, insecure with new poems, cradling moleskines and *Coastlines,* hugging our IPAs and arguing the pronunciation of *DeLillo;* loud talkers and outtalkers, first readers and frequent flyers,

The Fiddlehead's xeroxed slush pile under our arms as we lumber across Windsor Castle's back deck at 1 am for more beer money from the ATM by the bookstore, wilted twenties spat out from the bank loan aether while we stamp our feet and puff our own cold hoppy breath; or we lumber from the library at midnight after typing cramped papers on the poetics of birding; we lumber unsteadily down the winding walkway to the brick and finial gates on Beaverbrook, and then to downtown, to the Tannery, to our messy balled-sock apartments. And we lumber from Poetry Weekend's final hangdog reading, the burnt-dust smell of old rads still in our noses, Mem Hall's stained glass and mic'ed Poet Voice now a memory; we lumber down the hill with the news of who slighted who, who got too drunk, and we still love poems, some knocked us out, really they did, but no more poems for a little while, ok? Shane Neilson lumbers down the hill to a trunk full of chapbooks. Dan Renton lumbers down the hill in his fedora and Italian shoes. Jen Houle lumbers down the hill with her poems of Shediac, poems in Chiac, "Acadian ghosts / boring into the headpond." Tammy Armstrong lumbers down the hill, where at the Taproom we teach Ross our NBer talk: *that's right a good poem*. Brian Bartlett in the early 70's, high-school senior, kid poet of the Icehouse Gang, lumbers down the hill with Fred Cogswell. Lynn Davies lumbers down the hill. Bob Gibbs lumbers down the hill. Travis Lane lumbers down the hill to hunt review copies at the *Fiddlehead* office. Bliss Carman and Charles G. D. lumber down the hill in cape and spats, talking Shelley and planning canoe trips, their leather boots knocking tetrameter crisp on cobbles. We all lumber down the hill, almost falling, our feet leading us, Chucks and brogans, until we're poleaxed with the sleet sheeting off the mighty Saint John, "this fleeced and muffleheaded / snow blindness," and we try and try and try not to write another ode.

*

It's early fall at UNB, and in Mem Hall the particleboard tables are bowed with stacks of thin books; anxious poets shiver and smoke on granite steps outside, their vintage messenger bags sheathing really really nice pens. Upstairs band practice is ongoing despite the readings, the faint sound of an oboe curling down the hand-tooled staircase. The Quad's maples are lit red and match the buildings' Georgian brick. Here's a photograph of three young men at Poets' Corner, UNB's 1947 memorial to its Confederation Poets, the campus' literary omphalos; the cairn, weather-blackened at its bricked seams, backgrounds them: Shane Neilson in the middle, arms draped around Jim Johnstone and Marc Di Saverio. Shane's playing the proud NBer, the prodigal son returned, host to these Ontarians, and he's happy. They pulled in that morning, Fredericton's big blue water tower materializing on the hill.

Marc looks least comfortable in the picture, his full black suit hot, the strap of his bag pulling at his tie and jacket. I imagine the photo snapped after Marc's reading that morning, the first set, a reading where Marc yelled his poems under Mem Hall's neo-gothic proscenium. God—an awesome, awkward, beautiful and attention-demanding performance—"Go, my songs, verse through the ears of the smilers-in-their sleep, bridge them to their wakes. . . " I listened or tried to, and forgot about what pub we'd go to that afternoon and if they'd have the Picaroons IPA I really thought was fine. I didn't know if I liked his poems, but he cut through the verse-drift, the daydreamt dull stretches. But between poems there were proprietary snickers from the otherwise hushed audience, because Marc said his poems unselfconsciously, like he meant them. Shane calls Memorial Hall the Church of Poetry, with its porticos and cornices, quoined pilasters, its Miltonic stained glass. But Marc's reading was a different witnessing; this wasn't the way they worshipped here?

Critic Geoff Dyer says that the best photographs screw with temporality. Through some perceptual voodoo, they "seem to extend beyond the moment they depict." They can be heard, Dyer suggests, the photo's snapped nanosecond stretched in both directions. The Poets' Corner shot is hardly great. Standard Facebook fare. A record of a clear fall day. Yet let me misread Dyer and take liberties, stretch the moment to breaking. I see Marc losing his smile the instant the cell phone dispatches its ersatz click. He grabs a smoke from his blazer's breast pocket, turns, lights up while reading the oxidizing plaque on the poet's cairn, the bronze text sharp against regal red. He squints through his smoke, fingers scanning the names raised like braille.

*

I'm paging through my copy of *The Fiddlehead* 137, October 1983—the month I was born. The cover's a graduated off-yellow, what appears to be a deflated scarecrow on the front (title: "Machine II"). The design's simple, the colours hazy and sun-bleached. It's ugly in the way only eighties litmags are ugly. But I like it very much. I like it for this throwback ugliness, its textured paper, the endearing typo in the table of contents (both fiction and poetry are headed "Fiction"—there's "Fiction" and "Fiction"). I like it for its worn spine—not a crack but a deepening crease, hatched and uneven like a hand's heart line. The book's more rigid than newer issues—a crisp *twok!* in its flex—as if it's slowly hardening into its core materials, a ligneous fossil. I like it for its back section, *Atlantic Soundings*, a homey-toned and optimistic bulletin with regional announcements, pronouncements, news from the freshly formed Writers Fed, Alan (sic) Cooper presiding as first president. There's talk of their first successful event in the fall, a literary salon where "Premier Richard Hatfield paid an informal visit." Hatfield emerging from the gull-wing doors of a lime-green Bricklin SV-1. Disco Dick hanging with the poets: dig it.

I like it, too, for its feature on Alden Nowlan. Nowlan had died earlier that year, and here's "About Memorials," a short story where one of Nowlan's many persons named Alden Nowlan visits his hometown for a poetry reading and encounters the backward neediness of his birth place (a town called Balmoral, clearly standing in for Windsor, NS). The story's funny, vindictive and judgemental, a current of nostalgic love underlying the narrator's bristling. A parade of teachers and would-be mentors take the mic at his reading, claiming their part in his success, and the narrator complains bitterly, "What right did they have to create this caricature of me to give fictitious support to their self-esteem?" It's Nowlan berating all of us, future readers he resents and loves. It's Nowlan—master caricaturist—berating himself.

*

> Here in my living room
> are the twenty most remarkable
> persons in all the world.
>   —Alden Nowlan, "The Night of the Party"

Saturday night we gather at Ross's, cram ourselves into the hallways between rooms, crick necks as we look sideways at so many spines, bookcases in every room but the kitchen. The deck's for the smokers, disembodied cherries floating like fireflies on the arc of forced points. The bathroom lineup is too long, and we stand tight against the hallway to let people pass, drinks held to our chests like bouquets. The kitchen is the nexus, where the booze is, an archipelago of gossip and shoptalk coalescing around the centre island. Wayne Clifford asks me: "Do you want to hear the perfect poem?" To his snazzy and Blyish vest, I said: "Why not?" A short thing from Herbert I think— nice enough, but no such thing as a perfect poem. Tipsy and jostled, I smash one of Ross's fridge magnets, a small ceramic cactus. "It's ok. It was just from Arizona." This all to say that Poetry Weekend isn't just Mem Hall but Ross's, too— the dining room walls with their full run of *The Fiddlehead*, the living room and its quiet jazz and framed broadsides, that blue carpet like Nowlan's blue chair gone planar. That thin twisty iron stairwell, so Victorian-library. Shane's on the couch selling M. Travis Lane merch from the end table. We recite poems. Someone starts in with Larkin ("They fuck you up, your mum and dad.") but they're cut off: "Ah, everyone knows that one." I do "Skunk Hour" by the fireplace, sitting on the hearthstones with a half-empty case of Moosehead between my feet. The year before, I socked my Picaroons in the fridge and they were gone within the hour—thirsty, thirsty poets. It's warm, but this year I keep my beer close. On Sunday a hoarse-voiced Ross takes the podium and tells us he found a pint glass on the edge of his front lawn, stood upright as if carefully placed, filled to the brim with rainwater.

*

The party would've been at Alden and Claudine's. For sure. The poets filtering in, sitting at Alden's feet while he holds forth on the day's readings. He didn't like conferences ("The real writers write. The phoney writers confer."), but the weekend's slapdash organization and last-minute additions, its inclusivity and sociability, the unintentional theatre of the whole thing, would've appealed to Nowlan. Picture it: Alden still with us, in his eighties, his beard and hair white now, cumulonimbic. He sits with a half-filled whiskey and barely sips. Zealous grad students who hours before poo-pooed Nowlan for his sentimentality are lining up with their two volumes of the *Collected*, twelve-hundred pages. "Jesus," he says. "Too many poems. I'm not signing both volumes." But he enjoys himself this year, doles out honorary Maritime status with abandon. He gets his hackles up but once: "If you waste any more of my whiskey in that turkey-baster, I'll shove it up your ass." The poets keep coming through the front door, letting in the autumn draft. "You might as well put these down for a doorstop." He raises each volume of the *Collected* above his head. Arms thin, shaky. He's smirking. "*They'll* certainly hold the doors. Let people know all are welcome."

*

The book table's packed up. We've spent too much, shelled out just like last year. The dude we had a pint with was cool but now we're not so sure about these erasure poems. We're full of poetry, dyspeptic with it. We've nodded with lowered heads and crossed legs, practiced our relaxed attentiveness, a slouched languor in these unstylish chairs— our best listening pose. Some lines stay with us. Many we miss. We've waited patiently for the signal, the whispered *thank you*. We always applaud. I've watched poets stand in line at the book table with uneven stacks up to their chins, hundreds of dollars' worth, and they have the dogged look of obligation. We've signed our own books, crossed out our names on their title pages, replaced them with garishly illegible signatures. I asked about that once. The crossing out of the name. No one seemed to know.

*

There's a second party tonight, the Sunday weekend-ender, and we await our second winds. But now we're on stage, thirty or forty of us, and we smile for the group photo, its many takes, someone in the back always blinking, always cut off. One more, okay? The shortest up front, please. Behind us all, a baby grand gathers dust in the shadowed crossover. And we're all smiling politely, brought back to photo day at school, to tense family reunions. From the lit stage we stare at the staggered rows of seats. Aside from partners, supportive friends, the close-talking local who apparently just likes poetry, Mem Hall's darkened pews and folding chairs are empty. We're our own audience.

At a work training in Fredericton, I sneak off during lunch to haunt the public library archives on the second floor, a few rows of glassed bookcases opened with a key from the reference desk. I find *Alden Nowlan: Writer and Poet* (1984), an adult reader published by the Literacy Council of Fredericton, stapled and chapbook-thin. There are pictures throughout, cartoon line-drawings depicting pivotal scenes from Nowlan's life. I sense an attempt at socio-economic resonance, a presumptive connection with the book's inferred demographic. The simple syntax and grammatical structures are kind of beautiful, making this perhaps the most Nowlanesque of all writing on Nowlan:

> But no one told Alden what to do when he was little.
> No one told him what time to go to bed.
> No one told him what time to come home.
> No one told him to study.
> No one told him what to put on.

Each page is headed with its key sight words. Removed from context, these lists, their pedagogical randomness, make their own odd music—woods, logs, years, grandmothers, Nora, Old Em, told, home.

*

Ross appoints a Presiding Spirit each year at Poetry Weekend. There's no established rubric; it's a designation conferred for dedication, attendance, enthusiasm, distance travelled. I will never earn Presiding Spirit. I'm a wayward and fair-weather participant— missing years, knocking off Sunday mornings and heading back home hungover, shaky, missing half the readings. For two years during grad school, I lived in Forest Hill Apartments, cutting through a small wood to get to campus. Nowlan was buried just up the street. I never went to pay my respects.

*

Here's my favourite Poetry Weekend memory: I'm following a red pickup to Oromocto, the Saint John River somewhere to my left—Fredericton's outskirts dissolving into semi-ruralness, fallow fields, small convenience stores, the lowering sun pulsing through corridors of pine and birch. It's the Saturday of Poetry Weekend, the long break between afternoon sets, and Shane Neilson's taking me to his childhood home for an editing session on my upcoming chapbook with Frog Hollow, a small press he edits. We gather in the back sunroom, Shane in a worn lounger, and we lean over a coffee table with my sheaf of poems. In less than an hour, Shane dismantles habits, cuts lines, drops line-breaks, spends quiet minutes on single words ("how about *arbor vitae* here?"). He carefully and calmly makes my book a much better one. I put the marked-up pages away, and Shane's dad Doug makes us roast pork for supper—pulled and broiled in a roasting pan, the cuboid pieces seared black on their edges. Cream corn and mashed potatoes on the side. It's delicious. Right good.

*

At a reading at Windsor Castle years ago, students and their profs nod into craft beer and house wine as an author perorates with no podium to guard them. In the middle of a passage, their first novel's crux, a drunk pinwheels into the room, blasted and caroming off the tables. Someone stands to calm him. "It's a reading, man. Have a seat." This isn't part of the show. Buddy looks around, walleyed and pre-lingual, muttering in some dreamtongue. It's like he just woke up, or he's still in a nightmare, swaying in this living room retrofitted for a pub, like time's gone wrong and he's stuck in a loop, enacting some drunken performance from a Nowlan New Year's bash forty years before, walking the same drunkard's zigzag path, but there's too many tables here now, and who is that up front with the book? We've entered a Nowlan poem, but this isn't the exalted, exalting drunk of "A Certain Kind of Holy Man," one of "those who've learned / to sit comfortably / for long periods with their hams / pressed against their calves… contentedly saying nothing." This man is not comfortable. He doesn't know where he is. He doesn't know whose house he has been visiting all these years.

*

I pull up to 676 Windsor in Google street view's strange and slanted geometries. It's early fall, a blush of red on the front maple's crown. Thin leaf-cover on the gravel yard. The house is brick and blue-vinyl siding; it looks different from when Alden and Claudine lived there forty years back. There's a pic of the house from those days in that Nowlan NFB film. You know the film—the opening shot of Nowlan tapping a cigarette from his pack before he reads "The Mysterious Naked Man" in that stuffed-up voice, Nowlan in a dark shirt in a dark room and it's like he's a disembodied head, telling us all he's a congenital liar. Ginsberg reading "Britain Street," really selling it with the neighbourhood voices ("Brian! Marlene! / Damn you! God damn you!"). Each transition accompanied by a clarinet's atonal drone. Back then the house was simpler, all siding, surrounded by foliage like a house in the bush. There's shots of the interior in the film, too—low bookcases surrounding the living room. Is that the main bar area now? Did they take out walls? Still in street view, I swish frames to the back of the house, the lawn manicured, edged with cedar chips and topiary. Boxed ferns on the side path. I want to get closer, to climb the deck, see if it's open, but I'm stuck on Google's delimited and vectored track. Everything is silent and nothing is moving. The house elongates and stretches as I try to gain purchase on it, try to get closer. If only the

Google car's panoptic eye had caught someone leaving the house. Maybe they'd have a book. They'd be a blur of movement, two-dimensional and frozen, just starting down the hill. Lumbering.

TINDERBOX: DISPATCHES FROM THE VILLAGE OF FIRE

> *Burned to the ground*
> *means nothing's left*
> *but the need to say it*
>
> — Lia Purpura, "History"

My conjectured arsonist hurries through prewar penumbral streets, joyous, while oil lamps pulse like backaches through waved glass. He scouts unlocked barns and warehouses, carriage houses, shut up structures glutted with hay and raw timber, backing businesses on Kay and Main. My conjectured arsonist has an eye for aridity and wither, for bad ventilation and opportune vectors, can knock a wall's shake and feel how fast the wood might succumb, dance with oxygen, go up up up, transmogrify. Chemistry through instinct. He looks at the stars: so many cinders. He licks a finger, tests the wind.

*

We tally fires at the Legion, the County Fair exhibit hall, the public library's Heritage Week Community Social; we surmise, ballpark years. Hazy and half-crocked timelines.

"Oh, she's burned, what? Five times."

"Five? More, sure."

"Those two in the aughts, wha?"

We say "Yep" on a quick intake of breath, what counts for casual affirmation in the Maritimes. The local histories, pages held fast by the plastic tube of comb binding, constitute the not-quite-official record of spotty citation and anecdote. Arthritic fingers scan the lines. We slide photos from pH-neutral folders. We pour coffee from the Tim Horton's Take-12. But no one knows how many times Petitcodiac has burned.

"Now see that, there. That was my grandfather's store. She burnt."

You see the photos and assume it all burned. A denuded record in black and white, pen and ink. Fire the default for the no-longer-standing, even if there's no longer anyone to say for sure. We nod: She burnt.

Everyone in the village is a few degrees from conflagration. They had a long-lost relative who saw their business turn to foundation hole and charred girder. They can recite the second-hand accounts, the generalities. They sure as shit remember when Stedman's went in '93.

In *Village of Fire* (1997), authors Robert and Mary Hibbert bold all instances of the word *fire*, including adjectival variants like *fiery*. It's a stylistic choice that lends the book an insistent, obsessive edge. Your inner voice shouts *fire!* as you scan paragraphs—a mantra, an earworm, a warning. Even if looking for something else, fire foists itself upon you. Turn to chapter 12—"Fire, War and Fire" –and the fires ladder from the page, zigzagging down paragraphs, screaming from burning streets.

Hard to catalogue each fire; there's no definitive list. The histories on this point are fuzzy, contradictory, fire years blurring into one another. The Hibberts have it at nine to ten between 1859 and 1902, then major fires in 1913, 1919, 1925 (two), 1947, and 1993. That makes sixteen, by my count. While Hibbert & Hibbert place two major fires in

1925, Rogers[1] has only one, and in 1924 to boot. The earlier Burrows[2] starts with the 1868 fire at the Dunlop Spool Factory, then goes on to say Petty averaged a major fire *every four years*. He doesn't list them, assumes we'll trust his figuring. All three books agree that '13 and '19 were the biggies; Burrows bestows the *Great* epithet to both, and doesn't deviate. After reading through the accounts—exhaustive, often sporadic—I wish for an archivist of fire, a position passed down like a village scribe, an ageless official who tallies and knows the number, can tell you combustion rates, how fast each took the town, how long the smoke held in the upper atmosphere of outer townships.

They all mention arson. While Hibbert and Rogers tend toward the dismissive, Burrows really speculates:

> The most serious question, which might seem a bit far-fetched at first, upon deeper reflection causes one to wonder if perhaps for some bizarre reason there weren't just too many unexplainable fires to chalk up to coincidence. Is it, in fact, possible that a closet arsonist was plying his craft in Petitcodiac – perhaps even for decades?

There's this great bit where he dreams of hiring a specialist to investigate. Some part of me wishes that Burrows had followed through, got the municipality to pay a fast-talking gumshoe to knock on doors, trace the genealogies back to a culprit.

The histories paint the fire as predatory, almost sentient. It has agency; regularly referred to as an enemy that has "victimized" the village (Burrows), it caused villagers to be "constantly living in dread as to when another fire would strike again" (Rogers). Fire exists on the same moral continuum as the colourful characters these books detail. It is the village foe.

---

1 *Generational Memories: Life in the Village of Petitcodiac*, 2008.
2 *Petitcodiac: A Village History*, 1984.

But it's an old friend, too, a foil for their gumption. For the archive of Petitcodiac history—the photos and self-published books, the hearsay and handed-down talk—is defined through its many burnings-down. They triangulate the narrative of the village, hold it together. Burrows has "Fire" indexed 11 times, the most after "Blakeney"— the surname of the town founder. Local history is written out of the flames; a key plot point and a lodestone in the telling. Flash burns on the map.

*

My conjectured arsonist grows with the fires. Maybe there's fire in the blood, a generational pyromania. Maybe this is my conjectured arsonist's earliest memory: it's 1868, and he sits on an uncle's shoulders in a frozen field. They watch a small factory burn in the distance, stacked spools in the loading yard lit like trees, falling on their ends. Firewheels on the hill. His strongest memories are the rolling spools, huge bolted cylinders trailing light like something thrown by gods; and the heat on his face, too, bonfire-close except it was so far away.

"Look what I have wrought, nephew. I was catalyst, fire-carrier. Follow in my footsteps, for your father is a weak man and I'm Prometheus of a kind."

"Yessir." For what he saw was so beautiful, roaring like a storybook dragon. Like every wind rolled up since his birth.

*

One can use up memories, I've heard—advance a degradation through continual access. Neural pathways pilfered until there's nothing left. One takes too much each time. A stone, a leaf. A commercial block of corniced stores in sepia. Recollection as a kind of burning, using itself as its own accelerant.

Petitcodiac's past suggests mythic time, a cyclic relationship to events that have little to do with linear narrative. For one hundred years between the mid-nineteenth to mid-twentieth centuries, the continual burning of the village approaches the regularity of ritual. The same stores and buildings were rebuilt, over and over. A downtown resetting itself every few years, a perpetual newness. Nothing aged, gave itself over to typical causality. The fires collapsed time, and village history becomes relational, beholden to its fires—what was destroyed, what was rebuilt.

    I see the village slantwise; certain photographed places, specific blocks, come unmoored. A stretch of Main shows a dozen boxy storefronts, and I am lost in which iteration of the town this was. Which Blakeney General Store are we looking at, and when? No decades; just fire seasons. We're inundated with fire; everything ahistorical. Read enough about the fires, and the village undergoes a change, is reinscribed through fire. Our history books use the fires as guide and marker, but they do the opposite for me; I get lost when I try to date these sepia prints.

    Photos from the early fires—the big ones—are scarce, but the library holds a sequence of small black and whites documenting an aftermath: '13 or '19; maybe '25. They're unmarked, existing somewhere in the vague stretch of the early twentieth century. A few square inches of piled brick and busted framing. In the best of them, your attention's drawn to the top right corner: a lineman forty feet up a telephone pole, a sharp negative against the smoke's grey haze. He surveys the scene while a group stands at the foot of the wreckage, their bottom halves merging with the photo's darkened corner, so you almost have to squint to see them fully, figures half rubbed-out by fire. The photo is artful, the telephone pole's bisection off centre, adhering closely to the Golden Ratio. Most fascinating is how the photo frames an absence, a ghost of white haze where something once stood, obscuring all detail. Except for the lineman anchoring the viewer, you're adrift on the smoke, bereft, not sure what street you're on, from what angle the photo was taken, in what year. The photo enacts a loss of bearings, the bewilderment of a citizenry. The lineman's hip is canted, weight on one locked knee. There's grace to the posture: a trapeze artist at rest.

The lineman gives you hope. He's a symbol of the town's ability to start again. He looks capable in flat cap and breeches, calf socks and boots. Ready to work. In a minute he'll shimmy down the pole like he was born on it. He'll ask for a shovel.

But look closer. Our lineman just might be hanging his head.

Now your mind goes elsewhere, opens to a new geometry: the hip-bent body makes a triangle, a wide pennant signalling surrender. It's as if he knows it will happen again, and it will just keep happening.

Another photo from the library archives, but we're given a little more: a block of three shops on Kay Street. From what I can tell, the block sat exactly where the library is now. T. J. Drysdale, A. G. Parkin & Son, W. H. Pollock— simple brick storefronts, the only flourish the ball-top finial work on the roof. There's a blurred caption that reads *Block on Kay St. – burnt 1925*. The lettering is uneven. It's not kerning but a vertical problem, some letters higher than others, subtle derangement like a ransom note.

Burnt 1925: I like the odd grammar here, the lack of preposition, as if it's the year's proper name. *No one forgets Burnt 1925*. We could tack on *Burnt* to so many years in Petitcodiac's pyrotechnic 20th century. *Burnt 1902. Burnt 1919.* Do I trust this caption? How sure are we of the year? The decade? One long burnt.

*

A pale farmer's son, my conjectured arsonist. Useless in the fields, too sickly for the war effort. Most days he buggers off to play a hand-forged firesteel against chert stolen from an antique flintlock. He's in his secret place in the haymow, mesmerized by the sparks he makes. The brightness coning off the chert makes a negative on his closed eyes.

*

You'd expect more ghosts. Legends from the kids. Waxen Face in the upper windows. The Burned Man of Main Street, topcoat full with curlicues of birch bark, ash on the tip of his tongue. Names incanted over sleepover flashlights. Small town revenants roaming Kay Street, searching for the initial cause of their particular generation's fire. You smell smoke before you see them. So many possible sites—the slumping houses with peeling paint, the mansions of early lumber tycoons. Boarded barns on the outskirts. The Burlington Hotel before its 2012 levelling. Waterbury's Machine Shop that made torpedo casings during the war—apparently most of the works still stand, dust coating pinion gear and lathe, spider-webbed calipers and drill bits in the darkened corners. How has no myth condensed out of these closed-up spaces? But alas, no hauntings in the Village of Fire.

Among the library's archival holdings: a scrapbook of obits, its blue cover depicting man and wife around a hearth, their details blotchy and garish in 4-color saturation, highlights in a fungal greenwhite, like they would glow in the dark. They're looking at a scrapbook, supposedly this scrapbook; do they see themselves on the cover? They float in their easy chairs while fireplace brick disintegrates into the cover's twilight void. Inside, scissored column inches plastered to black cardboard, an almost complete record of Petitcodiac deaths from the 1950's to the late 1970's. They're written with that careful attenuation that characterizes the newspaper obituary, an anonymity that makes them both more distancing and more distressing. There's suicides and car accidents on Elgin's backroads, too many for a small town. Drownings in the Pollett River. The overexposed faces of children, their features washed out to shadowed brow and under lip. A photo of a prominent businessman's totalled roadster, all balled metal, and the accompanying caption says *Death Car*.

And no fire loses. Despite the exhaustive cataloguing of lost structures, the histories don't mention human lives. The townspeople seemed very good at egress.

*

His uncle bequeaths him his collection. My conjectured arsonist puts them in a grain sack and buries it by the riverbank. On lonely days, most days, he digs them out to turn them in the twilight. Ornate Dutch tinderboxes, all tracery and lace; a polished brass circular still stuffed with its original tinder fungus and punkwood. Some look like pots for camp stoves with their seared sheet iron, some varnished and inlaid like containers for holy books. His favourite is a plain eighteenth century English cottage piece, the one his uncle used, dovetail joinery rounded by use.

"This is my works, my tools and tackle. My paintbrush." His uncle is dying, feverish, a dry basin at his bedside. My conjectured arsonist sees blotchy linens, bits of lung clot in the folds. His uncle holds the English tinderbox above his concave chest and slides out its top cover. "You will use this too, godson. Now seek out dryness. I must sleep."

*

A tinderbox: anything that easily burns. A whole village, say. Every structure a tinderbox, tinderboxes replacing tinderboxes. The basic unit of a structure fire is the room. A fire moves from room to room, and a fire can end in a room, or just get itself going. Air flow, ventilation, material: the fire makes use of the room, its specific conditions of combustion. A fire can choke itself out, or gather heat for a backdraft, blowing out and up. Room by room, each its own open stove. At the turn of the century, balled newspaper was packed in walls for insulation. Surely there were fire headlines walled in those Petitcodiac homes, flaring as they turn to carbonized onionskin. Records of the village's last fire—not yet old news—becomes fuel to make the new one.

A hundred years later and I'm at the downtown crossing counting tank cars, ringing bells and flashing red from the beaked rail lights, my eyes ticktocking cylindrical brushed steel and matte black a few feet from my bumper, Procor, Procor, Procor, a million gallons of Alberta crude just passing through, perspective pinching them to a point on the tree line. So much potential fire. The Petitcodiac station was demolished in the eighties so there's been no passenger cars for decades, no stops, only pressurized combustibles on their way to the Irving refinery. In *Fire: A Brief History*, author Stephen J. Pyne brings up the paradox of contemporary combustion. The threat of modern fire "haunts every room and corridor... But open flame itself has virtually vanished. Like a black hole in space, fire has shaped everything around it without itself being visible." Boxed tinderboxes.

Wikipedia tells me that fire is an event, not a thing. Not a thing? A fire contained in a furnace, a room? A flint's spark? The wavering flame above a teenager's weed-leaf zippo? Surely, the Great Fire of 1919 was a thing for the locals. '86 was a thing. Stedman's was a thing. But the ephemerality of this idea satisfies: fire flares and goes out. Complex reactions concentrated in the *now*, impossible to store in the library archives. An event. A threadbare envelope of ash wouldn't suffice.

They mean that fire is made of things, not a thing in itself, and those things are oxygen, heat, and fuel—the three sides of the fire triangle. I find the fire triangle on Wikipedia, too, a graphic that might be prominent in an old boy scout manual. This equilateral triangle is surely simplistic, for every fire is weighted differently; they skew and stretch the shape, give it bent dimensions. The fuel side, I'd say, makes the long edge on a Petitcodiac fire triangle. Fuel: tonnes of lathe, stud, and hay. Dusty and drafty stores, their canvas awnings, everything rough-cut pine and dry goods. Barns sunbeat and sand-dry, empty except for a thousand cubic feet of oxygen and horse dander. A collection of tinderboxes, all in a row.

And now Werner, a local farmer, speaks of higher chemistries. Lasers and masers, a new fuel. Low-frequency energy beams causing ill health, killing his cattle. Top secret government gear undetected by modern medicine. Fire from the sky. Calfing in the off season. Strange tidings in the Village of Fire.

One day he's cutting wood on his property and a black ops helicopter is doing maneuvers over his fields. "They get me here, and right here." He points to his neck and side. "There's no wounds; no way to prove it."

I ask him why. He stands by the library's photocopier and tells me he uses traditional methods and shuns government subsidies, agrobiz, what he calls the gravy train. He knows their secrets, their methods of control, and they are trying to silence him. He talks of Art Bell, the New World Order, the Georgia Guidestones. Give a willing ear and he won't stop. He tells me to look at the bigger picture. The concentrated energy beams make us sicker. They control us and keep us complacent. Werner is angry and I have to tell him I can't talk about his theories when kids are in. Werner farmed the Old Country, and I only use the cliché because he himself used it unironically. Werner is shunned and looking for metaphors, and on quiet days at the library it's easy to follow him down the rabbit hole.

For Werner, the fire is poised, aimed, above us and all around. It's invisible and ubiquitous and therefore the worst kind. Tinder, all of us.

*

1919 is the year it all comes together, his masterpiece. The symmetry of the number. They're calling it the Great Fire. Just out of the Great War and now this: my conjectured arsonist watching them build again, his rucksack full of flint. He is a frowning tinderbox, tense, sinewy; he is August's seasoned cordwood.

*

The sign off the highway reads *Where the River Begins*: the town slogan, stamped on the baseball caps of town councillors. If we're being nitpicky, the Petitcodiac begins a bit upriver, meanders from Anagance before hitting the village. It rides the 106 through River Glade and Salisbury, widening, doglegged and silty down to Moncton where it's stoppered by the causeway, where scows and schooners once rode in from the Bay of Fundy, where the saurian bodies of man-sized sturgeon, all jaw and scutes, still wash up on its muddy banks. The village aligns itself with the river, the meager tourism of the river and the river's famous and shrinking tidal bore. The choice of water over fire.

This fall I hosted an eighth grade history class at the library; they came for bits about Petty, to shuffle through our archive for their reports, to fan out photos and yellowing correspondence. I hovered, helicoptered, concerned about tearing, theft, the oils from their grubby fingers, but trying all the while to act nonchalant.

"Who knows what they call the village?"

"Um, Petitcodiac? Duh."

"Guess again." I'm circling, pedantic in my patched wool cardigan. "They call it the Village of Fire. Yes. That's right. Because, well, it burned down a bunch." No one seemed impressed.

Who are "they"? I ask myself now. Like much else in the village, the nickname will degrade, burn away. Another fire event.

Still, and always, the best sunsets are mid-November, about four o'clock. From the narrowed perspective of the library's basement stairwell, through the glass door above, a watery coral over the baby blue and stairstep frontage of Corey's Garage. After locking up, each house along River Road is an outline punched through the bright firmament of a late autumn afternoon, leafless maples veinous against the sky's organ-pink fade. Atmospheric and molecular confluence. A bruise. Ablaze. Like the river behind them—or something even farther out of sight—might be burning.

*

My conjectured arsonist recites his litany, his liturgy: Mann's Meat Shop; Uz King's, Attorney at Law; the tailor shop, the barber shop, the boot shop, the harness shop; the post office, the confectionary; so many warehouses; generations of business-minded Blakeney's, their sundry stores selling sundry wares; Pollock's millinery, McRae's blacksmith, the old bank, the magistrate's; McCully's, MacKellop's, Hicks', Bickerton's, Lockhart's, Hurd's, and Yeoman's; Church and Co.'s general store, Innis' general store, Stockton's general store, Goggin's general store; the Mansard House; Smith & Dunfield's, Undertakers.

*

Petitcodiac is a quiet village; not much more than wind on winter Saturday mornings. Sometimes I pull off Old Post, jumping the decommissioned train tracks, and the downtown's deserted, postapocalyptic. The Foodland's diagonal parking spots like Main St.'s exposed ribs. Everyone is gone to town, see. I open the library and the deadlock's muffled click is the only sound within my perceptual radius. It's like I'm the only one left.

Petitcodiac only gets loud during fair week, when the population lines the roads during the Saturday parade, a small circuit that starts on Renfrew and goes up Old Post to cross Church, then back down Spring for a final triumphant turn onto a clogged Main—so many wide-brimmed sun hats and strollers, so many seniors in those big sunglasses that cover regular glasses. The whole village waving and cheering for the opening line of antique tractors, the show ponies, the flatbeds hung with helixed streamers. I drive the municipal half-ton, Bristol board and banners taped to the side panels pushing the Summer Reading Club, sunburned kids in the back. Foodland sells out of bottled water and the lines snake out for Hinchey Amusement's few cantankerous rides.

Now I've heard a house fire but once. My in-laws live beside an abandoned military base in Moncton, acres of yarrow poking through deteriorating concrete, a few spindly birch symbiotic with chainlink fence. One day we went out to greasy smoke on the other side of the lot, a few acres away, but our view was blocked by the trees. We heard it, though—the snap and bellow, a kind of sustained whooshing. A hearth with the volume turned up.

Just one house.

*

My conjectured arsonist watches from the iron trestle off Old Post. Horsetail cirrus glow orange with premature sunrise over the triangular block of Kay, Main and River Road—the downtown burning again.

There's church bells at 1 am. Insomniacs reading The Maritime Farmer *in an amoeba of candlelight get pulled from ads for art nouveau cream separators to shake awake their dreaming sons and daughters. Business owners with tin pails hunch like cat burglars on their roofs, cinders biting holes in their woollens. Wide-eyed as fire jumps to their neighbour's, sparks riding high on a northwest gale and licking.*

My conjectured arsonist felt his usual guilt and tried to join the bucket brigade, tried to follow the dopplered awooga of the pumper truck, brave men in peaked fire hats and double-button coats, half flung from the back handholds, the captain of Hose Company No. 1 high on the open front seat leaning into his turns. The rig and the men were brought in on rail, on a flat car from Moncton. Their hose-cart is pulled to the river's edge, two spindly wagon wheels and an axle intestinal with coil. The team axed through the ice and let out a thousand feet. No hydrants yet in Petitcodiac. They pumped all night and the downtown was doused with its namesake.

My conjectured arsonist ran against a tide of evacuees, ladies highstepping with lifted dresses, men still in long johns clutching the family bible, running towards the fields. Looters the only ones left—a basket of blue-ribbon quilts filched from a burning home, a man with a buckboard brimming with stolen goods, whipping his horse over the bridge, making it for Havelock.

"I can help. Please." *Firefighters wrestled hose to the frozen banks, faces squared shadow under curbed hat brim. My conjectured arsonist was elated; my conjectured arsonist was sorry.*

My conjectured arsonist floundered on scaly river ice, blue-knuckled, breaking the haft of a fillet knife trying to make a hole for the hose, but he wasn't thinking. They had an axe and a plan and man power.

"Out of the way, lad. Men are working!" *Surely they saw he was no longer a lad, that he was middle-aged.*

"Please please please," *to no one in particular. He saw redemption down there. Cold currents. Where the river begins.*

"Off the ice, arsehole! We've not the time to fish out a careless body."

My conjectured arsonist wanted to obey, but remained, for he was not strong enough to move furniture, would tire while digging cinder, would lose control of the woven firehose, ringing like a bell on its flailing brass business end. God. He knew these men.

After they pulled him off, he skirted the downtown—where the heat was so strong, a wall he couldn't climb over. And so he stands on the trestle bridge, his face cross-hatched with dawn shadow. Better to watch from a safe distance.

*

Fire has followed the village, creeped around its renoed edges. You'd think it's all history—vestigial bits from a hundred years ago, abstract. A spot of interest for passers-through. But fire is a contemporary phenomenon as much as village lore. Take the doozy in 1986, a spark arcing behind an old dryer in Howatt's Foodmaster; grey fuzz in the lint trap this year's tinder. Like so many times before, like almost every time before, it's a block on Main St. I get my info from newspapers the colour of ash, lumpy with the glue that holds them to a deteriorating Hilroy, a library donation years ago. Figures are tallied: 15,000 square feet, 4 businesses, 30 jobs, 70 firefighters, 2 million in damages. We're told that "the glowing fireball was seen up to six miles away in the misty night sky of rural Westmorland County." A photo spread shows a firefighter hosing down a pile of hot bricks at the base of a solitary chimney, an obelisk stuck in the middle of uptown. The sheet metal façade of Ella's Flower Shop, curled in on itself like a clenching hand.

One piece has it that while pressurized canned goods still exploded in the Foodmaster's blistering aisles, the owner's son was outside offering jobs to stock boys and cashiers. You see, the younger Howatt had his own grocery one town over. The group of them coughing heavy smoke, forlorn, hearing the zip of dripping plastics, and he's telling lit faces not to worry, there's room on his shop floor. And I have nothing cynical or snarky to say to this—a gesture I want to think is characteristic of Petty, a detail that threatens my ironic distance. So lovely, and kind of why I love this town.

Seven years later, a dumpster fire on Halloween took out Stedman's Store on the corner of Main and Old Post. Charges, the headlines tell us, slated. On Halloween fire gets legs—minor infractions, minor vandals out in droves, lighting the bush and minibarns. The RCMP, in the *Times-Transcript* from October 1993, boasts that Halloween is "our busiest time of year... it tops them all." Stedman's was rebuilt (everything always rebuilt)—red and white with a gambrel roof, one of the first shops you see when pulling into the downtown, a fibreglass sign on the front advertising the Westmorland Agricultural Fair. It's a Great Canadian Dollar Store now and there's still a dumpster in the back. We go on.

One day I'm in for Doritos and there's a box of 1991 Topps baseball cards at the cash:

> *10 packs for a dollar.*
> DO NOT EAT GUM.

Neat red wax paper, not crimped at the edges and seamed like modern packs but wrapped like little birthday gifts. What collectors call new-old stock.

"Where did these come from?" I ask. I'm faint, time-warpy. "Manager found them in the basement while doing inventory. Under a bunch of stuff. Imagine."

I almost bought some before I realized that I had never collected baseball cards, and was not at all nostalgic for the cards themselves but merely their context of display. The flat-packed and garish box on a store's front counter, the foldout signage built in, brought me back to elementary school trips to my neighbourhood Green Gables Convenience. And, furthermore, baseball cards probably aren't worth anything anyway, at least not those of the early 90s Topps variety.

Cross-reference the dates and you wonder if the cards were once Stedman's merchandise. The photo from the

Times-Transcript clipping shows a reclining firefighter hosing a rubble pit, a backhoe sifting the embers behind him. Could the cards have survived in some lost corner or bricked alcove of the Stedman's basement? Did early 90s wax packaging have unprecedented fire-retardant properties? Is this what remains? A quiet black box brought forth from the store's wreckage.

"Very cool," I say. "Might be worth something."

I kept my loonie and left with my chips.

A few years back, I opened the library after the weekend to find a blown window, hunks of superheated glass on the linoleum. Someone lit up a Saturn in the alley between the library and McPherson's Hardware; two stories up and the soffit like ribbon candy. The apartments above the store are still condemned. Word was the car's nylon interior was doused in gasoline that Saturday, a fireball off Main street, doors open like the spread wings of a Phoenix. No suspects.

In Burrow's village history—the most fanciful of the three village histories, and for that reason my favourite—the image of the Phoenix surfaces as he waxes poetic about Petty's glory, the town's get-up-and-go, its proverbial rising from the proverbial ashes: "Some might find it hard not to conjure up visions of that mythic bird when contemplating the number of times the small Village of Petitcodiac managed to pull itself up from out of the ashes of its own destruction and begin anew." There's much of this pulling oneself from the ashes in the histories. Perhaps it's the town's upright and practical religiosity—staid and forthright men and women shaking it off, trusting in providence, no time for legend, digging the mounting ash from their cellars, fresh framing laid and square before the smoke's cleared, smoke that still hazed the sun in outlying cattle fields.

McPherson's replaced the cooked red cedar lining the alleyway, yet they didn't go the length of the building, and you can see where the old and new wood meet. From the library's kitchen window, I look across to a seam of char on the side wall. Could be the contractor Mickey-Moused it, or they simply ran out of board: *good enough; pack her in.* Either way, I like it there, that difference. A few inches of sooty width, like a core sample's compressed line of carbon marking some forgotten catastrophe.

*

Let's linger with my conjectured arsonist. Here, on the ice. For he hasn't been routed from the river's surface yet, has not been dragged, limply, by Moncton's cursing fire department. He's ignoring their entreaties while the town burns around him. From above, my conjectured arsonist becomes some small splayed animal against the ice-dammed river, the thin Petitcodiac a calm blue vein in the red wound of surrounding fire—so much bright light and sound. He's cheek to cheek with cold that burns. He lets it infiltrate, its own fire turned into something deep and muscular. Prone, my conjectured arsonist thinks he can see movement below, subtle shadow and peripheral blue-black flickering—anti-fire in the late winter currents.

 "Christ Jesus. Just hope you don't see us off duty." The firefighters make a rough hole in the ice, and the surface vibrates with the steam pumper's work, the hose bucking with intake.

 My conjectured arsonist doesn't move; he distributes his weight. He remembers this detail—the distributing of one's weight—from an article in his school's one tattered issue of Boy's Life *adventure magazine. He does not know why he is so careful, why he is applying this particular survival technique, for he could not care less about falling through. Really, he watches the flickering below and wants to fall in, straight down, toes pointed. It would be a slowing down, everything exquisitely painful, an extraordinary enfolding where hot and cold transcend one another to meet at some embodied* limit. He would become a new inferno, carried downriver, the bright light of the Village of Fire behind him at last.

*

I've read railmen light the tracks on cold winters. When the weather drops, the steel can contract so hard it shears the joint bolts. There are modern ways to warm the rails—electric current, propane heaters—but lighting them up is still cheapest and most effective, what they've been doing since the dawn of rail travel

Petitcodiac on a dead-cold February. The populace has been hunkered for months on snowed-in farms, going feral, empty root cellars and a solid plate on the outdoor commode. Suddenly there's a flickering along Main that doesn't jive with fire's fickleness and tangled geometry. In rooms above the downtown businesses, heads lean out windows, bewildered at these parallel lines of light. Midwest tractor salesmen staying at the Burlington wonder if they came on the wrong week. They've heard the stories, Petitcodiac's other whispered name. But, look, so strange: it's not jumping the tracks.

*

My conjectured arsonist walks a beautiful promenade. Flames frame him on either side and he kneels to brush their twitching tips. They roll in slow waves up the rail turnout like the climbing arc on a Jacob's Ladder. Winter's coldest night, but my conjectured arsonist is warm between his fire lines. Normally he's hurried, harried; in daylight he walks the downtown flinching at his neighbours. Humanity's slow chemistry is a bore. There's no heat for him there; it's so hard to find a catalyst. Tonight his movements are graceful, fluid as flame. Anyone watching wouldn't see him, protected as he is by the light. He is a phantom. He is a king. These are the quietest fires he knows. But he's listening. They're trying to speak. They're leading him somewhere.

*

Can a geography be haunted by fire events, its soil primed for flame? Kay and Main has burned so. The library's oil furnace is a giant Hibernia, a green monster that rumbles like an idling pickup and covers the ceiling in tentacular ductwork. One duct vents to the men's room: the air gets fur-lined. When I turn up the heat on winter mornings, it sounds like something angry and nameless newly awoken. I enter the furnace room's clutter and dim—bald foundation stone seeping meltwater in spring, boxes of *National Geographic* and donated Louis L'Amour—and covering my hand with my sweater sleeve, I open the furnace's little scalding door, its edges filigreed with smoke's grease pencil. You can peek into its heart this way, a small circle rimmed with an asbestine material like unspun wool. The opening creates a curved occlusion that makes a squinting eye of the dense yellow light, a light that's pulse more than flicker. A small bit of sun. Before I leave at night, I tweak the bubble dome of the Honeywell thermostat—just low enough so the pipes don't freeze. But so much can go wrong, can kindle and consume; I know it now. This old building becomes a structure to hold my fire anxiety. I hope the blower fan is running smooth, that there's minimal friction. I hope valves open when valves should. I fear frayed wire, dust in the manifold. I need this sun contained.

GHOSTLY TRANSMISSIONS FROM JOHN D. ROCKEFELLER

ING'S

In January's 7 am dark the West Main Esso glowed like an insomniac's TV. We came in from Riverview off the causeway, slingshotted from the traffic circle, from our bedroom community, our warm suburban beds. Our Esso stood at the end of the line before Wheeler Blvd., Moncton's commercial terminus, a stretch of muffler shops and car dealerships, an Econo Lodge, a pub called The Salty Sea Dog. It sat between an Ultramar and a McDonald's, where the greasy sponge of an Egg McMuffin sopped up the beer I slammed at the night before's field party, Colt 45 through a hoodie drawstringed sphincter-taut to block mosquitos thick above standing water.

    A Chinese takeout behind us: a bungalow of cracked white brick once called KING'S. When I started at the pumps in tenth grade KING'S was ING'S, the roof's neon sign on the fritz. During my two-year tenure as gas attendant, as cashier, as stock boy, the letters kept going one by one until only G'S flashed us awake in winter.

    I was hired with a handful of pals, the boss the father of a school chum, my dad's golf buddy. We were middleclass kids without resumes, walk-ins with connections getting our two crisp shirts, the first shirts I'd tuck in. *You'll get a nametag next week.*

We came from a long line of teenaged pump jockeys—a proud heritage of postwar Brylcreemed boys from newly built suburbs, jumping from car to car lickety-split, captains of the modish sodium lit forecourt. Ten bucks Premium. Can you check my levels? No drip lines in our squeegee work. Start from the bottom and curve with each pass. Leave no streak.

We worked alongside full-timers that came and went, some there years before us, some sacked quickly for theft, for attitude: our wayward Team Tiger.

Now our Full Serve is gone, the outer island's glassed-in cash booth removed. Full Serve is a rare bird, the purview of rural outliers with dated pumps that ding their little bells, ring up their analog numbers like old slot machines. In the cultural consciousness, the gas attendant's now the gap-toothed guy in mechanic's jumper from the backwoods horror flick warning the road-tripping kids to git out, git out while they still can.

Were we the last ones? Post-millennials in their hover cars will never say Fill 'er up.

KING'S was ING'S and then G'S and now G'S is gone too, its alarm-clock red stuttering no more.

Dips

We'd rock-paper-scissors to see who'd do the dips, dreaded in winter: first task for the 7 to 3 shift to check the levels in the station's subterranean holding tanks. Except for the graveyards, there were always two to a shift and someone had to do it. Certain guys I could almost always beat, fool them by subtle gestures, make my hand look like scissors on two and switch fast to paper on three. But sometimes I lost. Sometimes I had to don the communal company coat over my regular coat, so cold I needed that extra layer even though the B.O. was criminal, chemical, a B.O. of accumulated years that went padding-deep, heightened by stale gasoline's sweet tang.

The dip covers were on the outskirts of the parking lot, edging the gravel berm of Milner, three raised circles half the size of manholes—blue for Regular, white for Premium, yellow for Supreme. The 3 to 11 shift now and then poured water on them before punching out; by morning I'd be stuck chipping ice with a tire-iron, wishing death on last night's duo. Once through, once each cover was wedged up, the locks were frozen shut: shackle, tumbler, and pins all seized, stuck fast in some solid-state physics caused by our North Atlantic cold fronts. Before the dips were even done, before I'd penetrated the tanks' frigid interiors, I'd be exhausted, half-frostbitten, indifferent to the fucking gas levels, the fucking dips.

When the holes were open I lanced our fossil fuel concern, checked its vitals. Esso's bread and butter was transubstantiated over eons—zooplankton dying in shallow pools among the dinosaurs, falling like dust in sunbeams then buried in sediment and ground by Earth's mortar and pestle, its prodigal tectonic plates. Porous things with complex geometry like snowflakes, pulsing jewels smeared to crude in 100 million years. The carbon ichor driven from our rubber-capped nozzles shared atoms with glassine creatures from Jurassic seas. A double burial: they brought it up for refining then put it back underground.

The dipstick was pole vaulter-high and notched off in quarter inches. The dipstick was stained and in need of replacement, its numbers blurred—was that a 3? An 8? Fuck it. Through the shaky incandescence of a dying flashlight, I'd fudge the numbers on a mouldy clipboard.

Lloyd (Team Tiger #1)

Lloyd was morbidly obese and walked from his apartment on Pine Glen for each shift, hoofing the length of downtown Coverdale—Riverview's main drag—and crossing the causeway to Moncton in orthopaedic shoes. He arrived damp and tousled, and took 5 in the back cooler to cool down, wheezing vapor among crates of stacked pop and Baxter's milk.

Lloyd said he'd only ever work at gas stations. Why? I don't remember or didn't care to ask. I trust Lloyd is working them still. I looked the few times I returned to West Main, peeped around back. Was he in the coolers? No Lloyd manning the pumps, no Lloyd on Big Mac runs. The station long ago switched owners, new management, the remaining staff transient anyway, the full-timers probably canned, the interior overhauled. Where's the Tim Horton's alcove? Where's Full Serve? Where's the old beige cashes with their tobacco-stained and stippled rubber keyboard covers? Where's Lloyd sitting on the small wooden stool behind the counter, framed by the back wall's technicolour cigarettes? The cigarettes are hidden, locked behind gray cupboards, and Lloyd is at some other station far away.

A Bag of Tapes, Cassette

A Sobey's bag frayed to macramé held our music, a collection hauled in by a long-time staffer sick to death of C103's hair band balladeers and rock country Republicans. The caseless tapes' white text was worn off from friction with other tapes, the tapes mostly metal: Hardcore, Grindcore, Power Violence, late 80s Thrash. Slayer's *Reign in Blood* and Cannibal Corpse's *Eaten Back to Life* backgrounded our transactions with the regulars, customers in for Skoal and

Double Doubles cocking eyebrows at the tinny aggression from our communal boombox on the ledge.

"The fuck is that?" they asked.

"Napalm Death."

"Jesus. Throw on some AC/DC."

The left deck was stuck shut with a jammed Memorex. I like to think it was always there, unplayable but vital, unfit for our teenage ears, ghostly transmissions on its magnetic tape, a palimpsest of deceased employees and boardroom stake-holders, oil barons, the static-crackled voice of John D. Rockefeller speaking in tongues from beyond his Ohio grave, his obelisk, intoning Standard Oil's initials like some vague prayer for the future: *SO, SO, SOS . . .*

Jim (Team Tiger #2)

I worked with him on Christmas Day while the customers lined out the door, our Esso the only place open with Tim Horton's. *Gotta get my Timmy's.* Customer after customer telling us, *Brutal. Morning shift on Christmas. But I gotta get my Timmy's.* I wanted to be home, I wanted to scream at everyone to go home. I wanted to close up, snuff out Esso's eternal tube fluorescents. But Esso's clinical blues shut for no one.

Jim's parents owned companies, his older brother a famous brain surgeon. Jim was the black sheep, cut out, cut off, plagued with schizophrenia he blamed on bad acid at a Pink Floyd *Division Bell* show.

"I was never the same. I remember the light show and then: hospital."

Jim was okay with working the Christmas 7 to 3, had volunteered for it. "I don't mind. Had Christmas already I guess." Jim talked slow and moved slower. "I got this sweater," he said. His tow head and blank eyes. I had many,

many presents waiting for me at my house; I had my smiling folks and my older brother home and I was missing morning mimosas and a fat Butterball going gold-leaf in the oven.

Another night Jim was desperate for smokes and called up Esso while I was working: "Spot me a pack of smokes. Just a twenty-pack. I'm dying. I'll give you my *Dark Side of the Moon* on vinyl. Early pressing." He met me under the awning with the record as promised and I gave him a fiver for his Export A.

Jim was always trading, trying to hock what little he had. A friend who worked there went to Jim's place to buy a poster (again, Pink Floyd) and found a single mattress on the floor, a busted dresser, a nightstand empty except for a buck knife.

The same friend ran into him at Wal-Mart years later. Jim was in full Wal-Mart regalia, pinned blue vest and price gun. Eye contact was strictly avoided, different aisles picked, but they caught up in Houseware.

"This isn't really what I do," Jim had said. "I'm undercover for the government. Don't tell anyone."

A Bag of Tapes, VHS

Mescaline Chris, a loyal customer, bragged about the drugs he ran, the shit he capped in pills, what he cut it with. He'd come in for free Tim's (we rarely charged the regulars), for talk about his kids. He kept saying I'd be an astronaut, was sure of it.

"I'm going to school to study astrophysics," I said. "I'll never go to space."

"Whatever, man. Spaceman shit."

Mescaline Chris had something to show me in his car one night. His Bondoed hatchback parked at Pump 1.

"Come check this out." He waved me over. His grin out the rolled window.

I went over, got in. It was a slow night.

At my feet in the passenger seat: a black trash bag of porno tapes, their display boxes larger than the everyday slipcases, a bigger format from the dawn of rentals—more square-footage for back cover skin, lurid angles.

"Ten a tape."

I reached in, held up *Ass Attack 8*. What had changed since *Ass Attack 7*? What new innovation in camera work, in body plan?

And where did they come from? What store was held up, what creep's dim basement looted? I remembered Midnight Video in Riverview Mall, one of the last establishments not steamrolled for call centre space. Midnight Video had a back room through blue saloon doors; we'd sneak peeks as kids on Nintendo runs—flashes of pink and costume kitsch in the glare. Did this pilfered smut come from Midnight Video? Was Midnight Video gone by then?

"Classic shit here. Ten a tape. Three for twenty-five."

Mescaline Chris' hatchback bled bad vibes, the air dense with something recently gone wrong.

"I'm good," I said.

I made my escape. I had the Internet anyway.

Alan (Team Tiger #3), or, Bathroom Key

A variation of the same from every customer we gave it to: *Could use this as a weapon, bro... Shit. You could kill someone with this.* And there's some truth there: the bathroom key was zip-tied to a sawed-off broomstick, all electrical tape and foot-long menace, a germy nightstick waiting for the right tweaked cro-mag to take it to the wrong party. Alan used the key as exercise equipment on quiet nights, a device invented more out of boredom than physical enrichment: 2-litre Pepsis tied with rope to each end for a kind of close-grip forearm curl, bottles raised and lowered slowly throughout our drawn-out night shift, hundreds of times, as Alan watched his form in greasy windows.

Alan was resourceful in other ways—for snacks he'd crack a package of hotdogs and cook them in coffee filters on the Tim's machine's top burners, beige plugs of nitrates browning in white flowers. These being gas stop wieners, convenience store dogs way past their display date, E. coli doggers. Who buys hotdogs at an Esso?

If the bathroom key never came back I'd assume its final end as evidence: the forensic team's filed photograph, the checkered crime scene ruler. Blood spatter in the corner, a tuft of hair stuck to its tip.

Chris (Team Tiger #4)

A different Chris, not Mescaline Chris: we'd catch him out the window walking down Main, late for his shift, trucking it with set jaw like a wrestler entering the ring, like Stone Cold, whom Chris liked. Chris went by DJ Taz and had the tattoo to prove it: a botched and blotchy likeness of the Warner Bros. character on his bicep, its shaky lines like Sharpie on Kleenex.

"A buddy does it out of his apartment," he said. "Didn't cost shit."

Chris the compulsive liar, Chris who tried to convince me they made special CDs only DJs could get, discs you could scratch like vinyl.

"I don't think CDs work that way, Chris."

"Yeah man. Got little grooves in them for your fingers." His napkin diagram looked bulbous, convex, nothing like a CD.

Chris was in his mid-twenties and his wife seventeen. One day he showed up crisscrossed with facial scratches, his uniform breast pocket torn wide open: a gaping mouth revealing a darker blue underneath.

"Me and the wife got into 'er. I hit her once, she spun around twice then hit the floor." Eyes all boyish glee and feral rage. He twirled his index finger then jabbed downward: how she spun, how she fell.

She was my age and I kept seeing her post-hit, spinning and spinning.

We found out Chris died in a drunk driving accident during our first year of college. A call from the boss to his son; most of us were there together: same college, same residence. Like Esso again, like high school. I remember one buddy drunk on vodka, stomping the floor of our room: "How's Hell, Chris? How's Hell?!" We all laughed, safely ensconced in our dorms with our care packages, our parents' cash transfers, our futures bright screens of potentiality, pockets deep with loans not yet blown.

We had a laugh then got our hands stamped. Student night at the Gorsebrook.

Mayflies

Every spring the mayflies were upon us with Old Testament fervour. They bred on the stagnant banks of the Petitcodiac, unzipping their larval coats in synchronous emergence to cross Main at dawn, a smoke of primitive bodies alighting on our Esso for a few days of sun, of brief life. The station's steel façade turned to a rough mat of wing, arched abdomen, and two-prong tail that rippled with each breeze off the water. Saturday found me determined with broom, taking wild sweeps at the east side wall and retreating in disgust. Sweep, retreat. Sweep, retreat. Avoid those pitchy screams we reserve for when insects touch our skin. I normally liked the broom, liked sweeping the parking lot at night, sweeping places that didn't need sweeping, Discman-clad under the summer sky and the station's bright awning, everything lunar: I was the last person on Earth.

But now I was disturbing fragile life cycles with my beloved broom. The mayflies rose up in indignation, clicking audibly, from some evolved fear-mechanism or from a dense clattering of exoskeleton, I couldn't tell. I swept up the ones I'd downed, my dustpan deep with mashed thorax.

The mayfly has a midlife phase called the subimago, a developmental limbo between naiad and adult. I too was a subimago cursing through my liminal phase, man-boy unsure of who finally owned this parking lot, us or them. But I did what I was told. I rushed the walls and swept up their fallen brood and dumped them into our hexagonal garbage cans until the walls were their dun silver once again.

TYMPANA

Billy Joe screams into a grasshopper.

*

I say *into*: sound as enveloping medium, sound finding the insect's hollows, its spiracles.

*

He makes an amphitheatre of cupped hands. We are eight. He yells and yells.

*

A vibrating exoskeleton in a universe of sound.

*

Billy fights the new kid. He is a recess tussler—stretched crewneck, permanent grass stains. Yanked aside in the mudroom, snot-nosed and bloody. *Say you're sorry.* His only tears are crocodile.

*

And they *can* hear. Like most insects, grasshoppers have a tympanum, a rudimentary ear behind the back leg. The tympanum is a sensitive organ, used primarily for mate selection.

*

Mandatory to fight Billy because he's the strongest, the top in our flawed and unspoken grade school ranking system. He and the new kid grapple by the sliding hill for most of lunch while the circle of onlookers slowly diminishes. Only then is the new kid allowed to eat with us.

*

We have one—the tympanic membrane, the eardrum.

*

The newswire says *transient in nature*. He lives in his black van and he's on the run—wanted for death threats, violating parole. Something about a protection order. And our old crew are sharing the wire, sending it around. *Holy shit. Is that him?* And how unsurprising, almost boring. Another bully that grew into the same. We shouldn't be bored by this. But we shrug: *Of course. Like, of course.*

*

Billy's anger funneling down, going deeper than the inner ear.

*

Lick the dirt, he tells Rich. Rich on his knees by Claude D. Elementary's packed marble patch: a supplicating look. *Do it. Lick the fucking dirt.* And he's going to it and he does it and then that bullying cliché: no one says a thing. We laugh, for we aren't the ones on the ground.

*

I just can't see him putting the grasshopper back, placing it gently on a blade of grass. No way.

*

There's three of us, bored, sitting on the lawn, ball gloves forgotten, and he tells my friend his sister will get pregnant.

Go ask. When she's due. We are eight. She's eleven, twelve. The rules here are uncertain, we have no rubric. *Just go and ask her. They all get pregnant.* Why does he need this? *Ask her, man. When she's due. Ask her when she's due. Just go ask her.*

*

I study the mugshot, not because he looks different but because he looks so much the same. The first I've seen of him since middle school. The same but some change in angularity, a subtle deepening of contours. Square jaw, butt chin. He looks like any bro that would end you for looking too long in his direction. He looks like twenty years ago; and I could say the difference is that violence has become worn on the face, a migration outward. Probably just a trick of context, how a mugshot skews toward haggardness. Probably just age: a violence done to every face.

*

Incomplete metamorphosis: where the grasshopper nymph looks just like the adult.

*

Billy had older brothers, men to us, iterant and shadowy figures from previous marriages that came to crash for a bit—custody-sanctioned visits, military furloughs. Sometimes they had a bedroom—glimpses of centerfolds and metal posters from the hallway—the stringy corpse of Eddie the Head clutching a Union Jack, the bloody mallet from *Kill 'Em All*.

*

We sing a duet in the school Christmas pageant, Billy and I. We wear dress shirts and paper donkey ears. Animals at the inn.

*

During food scarcity, the two-striped grasshopper (*Melanoplus bivittatus*) may become cannibalistic.

*

Mock War in suburban dusk—hide-and-seek with teams and secret codes, makeshift prisons and light torture. We hide under decks, under backyard pines—elbows on mats of fallen needles while we watch for marauders under our streets' high pressure sodium lamps. We hide in the plastic tunnels of Goldsboro Park's jungle gym, marker tagged, miasmic with piss from drunk teenagers. We hide in new construction's skeletal framing, in the open basements of poured foundations, our subdivision growing out into our woods and ATV trails. We seek each other out in ravenous groups. We pry up a manhole cover—hollow throatiness of metal over asphalt—so Shawn can hide in the sewer system beneath Carnation Crescent. And he holds the tunnel's iron rungs throughout the game, waiting it out while each of us gets caught, roughed up, and then we finally let him out, sole survivor.

*

The dreamt grasshopper is associated with freedom, independence, spiritual enlightenment.

*

One Mock War winter Billy's stepbrother stalks us in a snowstorm, his judogi tied over a skidoo suit for camouflage. Steve is legendary for fights at his old school. He has a temper and does freeweights in Billy's basement with concrete plates covered in plastic. Steve is stealthy and Steve wants our blood. He will be a cop or a soldier or a mob enforcer one day, something martial involving extreme power dynamics. He needs our code and he will hunt us down. Those picked for his team are thankful, go where he goes. Steve catches one of us in the overgrown path across from Claude D.

Elementary, hip-tossing his prey onto the frozen mud. *The code. Now.* Steve is calm, hardly winded. F*uck you. Fuck you. Never.* And, true, we may not give it up, and maybe he will manhandle us back to basecamp by the park. But eventually it'll be over—we always give the code in the end—because we are tired, our mouths bloody; because Billy Joe's stepbrother will take Mock War's manufactured brutality too far, and we will be called soon for supper, thank God.

*

The van's in the newswire, too. A stock image, cribbed from Google, the dealership's slick booklets—touched up so it looks liquid, front wheels slightly turned, all display, arcs of light caught in the curvature. Sleek. New car smell. Billy's van would be different, though, so far from that. Dinged up from driving the back roads of Red Deer, running from his crimes, mud fanning from the wheel wells.

*

Since starting this, I'm seeing grasshoppers everywhere. Somehow, I missed them all summer. After bringing in groceries, one clings to the roof of my car. Another against the house's siding: so still, caught half frozen on a late September morning. One upside down on the driveway, crushed wing, thorax trailing viscera, forelegs slowing playing the air.

*

Steve splits Billy's Strat-style Yamaha up the middle. I don't remember the reason but I remember the purest rage I think I've ever seen when Steve swings the guitar over his head—wields, brandishes, I need a verb of ancient weaponry, Norse berserkers—plastic glaze cracking, body reformed as it comes down on the basement's carpeted cement, spilling wired knob and pickup. Billy cries and it's like seeing your parents cry—awe in the sheer rarity, the wrongness. He sits there and cries among the splinters. Billy Joe made other kids cry.

*

To be eight. To dilly-dally. To keep a kicked stone going. To pick at the black ropes of tar sealing McDowell's cracked asphalt. To run a stick along a fence. To fence in. To wake terrified of an opened closet's hung shirt. To think the world might end when you go to bed. To call home at sleepovers, shivering from an unfamiliar room, coat over pajamas, hoping no one wakes up, Bloody Mary at any moment will emerge from the black lake of the basement's full-length oval mirror. Billy will call you a pussy at school, but the relief you feel when you see headlights at midnight's door, when you're dozing in the driver's seat, carried home.

*

Could the grasshopper hear his frequency?

*

There's always the kid that knows more of sex and violence in grade school—play fighting a little too hard; the way they'd lock their hands with yours, palms together, to make a vagina with the skin between thumb and forefinger.

*

Billy Joe screams into a grasshopper and the tympanum vibrates to breaking.

*

Tympanum (Arch.). The triangular space between the horizontal and sloping cornices on the front of a pediment in Classical architecture; it is often left plain, but is sometimes covered with sculpture. This name is also given to the space immediately above the opening of a doorway, &c., in medieval architecture, when the top of the opening is square and has an arch over it. (A Concise Glossary of Architectural Terms, 1846, John Henry Parker.)

*

Billy Joe screams into a grasshopper and isn't heard at all.

*

The newswire says *do not approach.*

*

In 1130, Gislebertus completes *The Last Judgement*, a tympanum above the entrance to The Cathedral of St. Lazare in Autun, France. To the right of Jesus, souls rise to the Kingdom of Heaven; to His left, souls are weighed—the pokings and proddings have already begun, demons with wide downturned mouths like Greek tragedian masks.

*

An abusive relationship, maybe: death threats over the phone. Violent texts at work. *Bitch you're dead. Lick the dirt.* I don't know any of this, don't know the particulars—why he's wanted, why he is living in his van, why the gun—but I concoct stories, and they aren't my own.

*

Inscription along the bottom of *The Last Judgement: May this terror terrify those whom earthly error binds for the horror of the images here in this manner truly depicts what will be.*

*

We're given a tiny mugshot—bleak light and bleary eyes— and we go from there.

*

Lick the dirt, he tells Rich in grade two.

*

May this terror terrify.

*

Sourcebooks for Our Drawings

Like much medieval art, the Tympanum at Autun is cramped with figuration, its carved stone details all forefront, the figures gangly, extraterrestrial. Contorted sinners, heads in bands. A gigantic Jesus front and centre, His bent skeleton limbs like the long hindlegs of a grasshopper.

*

Our elementary school yearbooks were squat softcover booklets, our pictures in blurred black and white—awkward in our poses, our postures.

*

The images here in this manner truly depicts what will be.

*

To compare his mugshot with the grade two yearbook—gauge just how much has changed.

*

In my backyard frog pond, Billy and I catch a water tiger in our plastic net—the segmented, shrimplike larvae of a diving beetle. We spend the afternoon feeding it the speckled tadpoles of northern green frogs. Squatting at our 5 gallon bucket, we're entranced as it sucks writhing prey paler and paler, curved pincers injecting dissolving enzymes, clamped to the tadpoles' bulbous front ends; and the water tiger drinks them until they're ragged wisps, torn plastic bags floating in yellow pond water. We don't yet know what it is, but we will feed it whatever we have. We would feed it all day long.

*

A standoff in a Camrose 7-11: the van's surrounded but it will be two hours before Billy tosses the gun. Was there a negotiator? Bullhorns? What would they want him to hear?

*

One of the damned in the Autun Tympanum appears to be gripped at the head by giant disembodied hands—the water tiger's pronged mandible.

*

When Billy Joe dropped the gun, did he wish for a manhole to hide in? Does a gun on asphalt sound at all like a manhole cover?

*

I don't want Billy Joe trying the pellet gun. It was my father's, something he saved for with caddying tips in the mid-sixties, lay-away at the five and dime. He gave it to me for Christmas, with ceremony, handing down its long frayed cardboard box. I practice in our basement, halving a pencil crayon at 30 paces. *Give it over*, Billy says. But I don't want to give it over because Billy Joe with a pellet gun means broken skin, loss of vision. I give it over like I don't care, like, nah, I'm not worried. He aims low, shoots me in the foot—a red pinhole on my heel for days. A bloodshot eye, a mugshot.

*

Decades later Billy hides in Western Canada's second growth forests, gun in the glove box, awaiting his showdown.

*

Water tigers will eat things bigger than themselves.

*

We play Mock War, trespassing under front porches, vigilant through latticework. We are scared; we have the code and we'll be damned if we give it up.

*

How do we hear each other?

*

An amphitheatre of cupped hands.

SHELF READING

The Petitcodiac Public Library's Canadian poetry section spans 19 inches of shelf space: the 819.1s in Melvil Dewey's decimal system. When I started as Library Manager in this New Brunswick village three years ago, I was curious; I write poems myself so I wanted to see what verse was stocked in my new home-away-from-home.

The library's in the basement of the Masonic Lodge, off Main and beside the Legion. You go downstairs to a single room of packed square footage, shelves sardined with collections born of necessity, whim, demand, and chance. Before we took it over, the space was used for community auctions and sock-hops. We came from the old bank in the early aughts, the books brought over in the municipal backhoe's front loader.

The poetry books take up a lower shelf in Nonfiction, ensconced in a plastic adhesive the library biz calls Tacky-Back (value death for collectors). There's a fair sample from Canadian poetry's doldrums—garish covers spanning two decades, 70s to 90s, each chock-full of mostly low-watt free verse. There's a good chunk of early Atwoods, one called *You Are Happy* (Oxford University Press, 1974), the title writ large in a hippie's chubby VW Bus font. There's *Bursting Into Song: An Al Purdy Omnibus* (Black Moss Press, 1982), a Gary Geddes called *The Acid Test* (Turnstone Press, 1981). There's a Ken Norris called *To Sleep, To Love* (Guernica Editions, 1982), the author pensive and shaggy on the cover. Here's some positively head-spinning stuff from the opener:

> When you are gone
> I am alone, there is
> no one here beside me. ("The Differences")

There are unexpected gems that haven't been dusted in decades. We have Irving Layton's *The Darkening Fire: Selected Poems 1945-1968* (M&S, 1975), the card last date-stamped when I was a toddler. It could've gone out after our library system went digital, but I have my doubts. There's a 1995 chapbook from West Coast poet and editor John Barton (*Destinations, Leaving the Map*, above/ground press, one of 100). How did it get here?

We also have *News and Weather: Seven Canadian Poets* (Brick, 1982), edited by August Kleinzahler, from his days north of the 49th. Only seven poets! The flame war such flintiness would spark today! The incredulity at who was overlooked! The accusations of favouritism! Of cliqueishness! Kleinzahler's half-page forward is refreshing in its bluntness, its refusal to polemicize. No 30-page clarion call here, just a humble offering: "Here are 7 poets I read and listen to with delight. And envy." Kleinzahler includes early A. F. Moritz, his dense metaphysics there even then, though less apocalyptic than erotic:

> A black orchid convokes bees
> at your body's centre,
> a stem of urine
> connects it to the ground.
> Beside where you stand, the fishes

> leap up an arc of light
> and hang in a rainbow
> over the disgorging cleft. ("Black Orchid")

My circ system says we once had David Solway's *Selected Poems* (Vehcule, 1982). I like to think it was thieved by some disgruntled high school English teacher, done with slogging through the backwoods of the CanLit unit and ready to preach the undervalued. Solway, a poet with no time for the shallow regionalism and civic-mindedness of most Canadian verse, would have appealed to my imagined educator. I picture an arrogant recitation of the cheesy "Lampman Among the Moderns" to a classroom of beleaguered AP students:

> Canadian poets, learn your craft
> and celebrate the hundredth draft.
> Scorn the sort who stumble into print
> and excel by grace or accident,
> or ply their patriotic pens
> to show they are good citizens....

But I romanticize. A likely end: Solway's book boxed with Harlequins and driveway-bound on spring cleaning, its plain and sow-pink cover curling in the rain.

Must I tell you they never go out? That they're passed daily by patrons on the way to Knitting or True Crime?

But I try. I do. Every April I air out the choice bits; I fan them on my display table above a poster advertising Poetry Month. Alas, this doesn't much help. They remain stationary and unthumbed throughout this cruellest of months, their cheap paper's lignin breaking down to a deeper yellow.

On first encounter, there's something inherently diminutive about a row of shelved poetry. Unlike the pure tonnage of bestsellers standing at military attention, their thick spines projecting shiny caps, poetry books compress to a wash of pancaked indistinctness. They're wisps, quarter-inch spectrum bands of dull colour, loathe to call attention to themselves. To the idle browser, they promise little.

The locals know Petitcodiac as "The Village of Fire," the downtown core razed and rebuilt multiple times throughout the late 19th and early 20th centuries. This summer, kids lit up an old Saturn next door; they left the four doors open, interior sopping with accelerant. The heat blew out a window in the library's kitchen. I came in on Monday to charred curtains and glass crystalling the shag on our stacked institutional chairs. The perps are still unknown, the town left to its own theories: a tryst, a drug deal gone wrong.

If one day my block catches again, and I see smoke, I'll take what I can. After the tatty banker's box housing the village archival material, I guess I'd go for the poetry. I'd fill my arms and run through the flames, a cavalcade of slim volumes cartwheeling behind me. I'd bring them upstairs and out into the light.

A FIELD GUIDE
TO NORTHEASTERN BONFIRES

>There are many ways to be transfixed, and no season is safe. If it is winter you may be transfixed by ice; if it is springtime, by fire-finch music or phoebes singing or the squeaky compositions of fox kits. And if it is summer, you may be transfixed, like Dryope, leaf by leaf, by clambery vine-winding love-bind. For love, onslaught-love, beleafs all things.
>
>—Amy Leach, "Love"

>It may be stated that all children, by definition, are explorers, and that to discover the camel is in itself no stranger than to discover a mirror or water or a staircase.
>
>—*The Book of Imaginary Beings*, Preface to the 1957 Edition, Jorge Luis Borges, Trans. Norman Thomas di Giovanni

Bonfire

1

The bonfire dies to make its nest, the result of a nightlong burning—the carbon pit, layers-deep, it builds up for offspring. A nest is countless deaths, one site marking generations. The morning reveals slow efforts—a circle of ash, bottle caps erased of their logos, the night's last birch worn to a black river stone, thrown on at 4 am by an uncle trying to keep the party going. The bonfire, even the most spectacular—gas-fed and throwing ten-foot flares, eating that year's spring cleaning, legless furniture and barn guttings—even those plasmic monsters rarely last a night, like insects beholden to some fleeting life cycle. They are burnt offerings to themselves.

2

Bonfire generations tend to stay put, built on top of each other like churches. Yet they are hungry for the overhang—this is how they might propagate and grow, pupate into something unwieldy. For a bonfire is really just a flickering potentiality, the juvenile stage of something much larger. They lick and jump at the undersides of leaves, sending their sparks up between branches, a small bit of lit bark or newsprint—their ashen seed tunneling upwards, following the stars' diurnal motion.

3

Regarding bonfire calls, the experts know much. Upwind, the best-tuned ear can tell a Stone-lined Whisperer from a Field Party Rager, a Northern Summer Camp from a Suburban Leaf Eater. They know the language of crackle and hiss, of low roar; can match the amplitude of each vapoured pop to its species of wood. Each conifer's bough, whether White Pine or Douglas Fir, projects a different fizzle. Approaching a night field's far-off spot of light, a bonfirist can pick its cracking song out of the wall of spring peepers, can tell if it's gaining momentum or dying slowly, if its buzzed stewards gorged it with chainsawed hunks, or if they've stumbled off to let it consume itself. The experts know the calls; they can prove it. But *The Field Guide to Northeastern Bonfires* has yet to be written.

4

Their grandfather was a principal once, and he gets them to make schoolhouses. The cousins find cardboard boxes they fill with uneven windows—squares divided into four smaller squares. Each writes their school name at the top, and if some of them even like school, and for whom the idea of their school burning down causes some anxiety, for whom this schoolhouse-burning may represent a tempting of fate, they don't let on, for part of them loves the conflagration, always too quick—the box placed carefully open-side down on iron rods welded to the top of the firepit's cut barrel. After all, this burning of schoolhouses is the farm's fireside ritual. Flames get the inside first, smoke seeping from the cardboard's folded seams. Tentatively they seek out the front, push up the sides, expose the corrugation underneath. Rapt, the cousins watch flame kiss the markered window ledge—too soon, too soon, the crude teacher yelling out the window, a comic balloon *HELP!*, stick figure arms reaching toward the sky.

Bracket Fungi

Conks. Turkey tail. The spruce's many ears. The cousins snap them from the trees—fanlike protuberances like cockle shells. They look soft, but they're as hard as the wood they clung to. Tops layered like a river's muddy banks. Their grandfather gives the cousins permanent markers to decorate the smooth undersides, where the spore was once released. They draw family portraits, suns with radiating black lines. They write their names. They draw shaky rainbows, thick lines following the fungi's arch.

Bridge

1
Some say the bridge predates the road; some say that it's always been there. Despite its apparent solidity, the bridge is all chemical reaction and capillary movement—the underside's wider fissures grow their fungal efflorescence, tooth-like, the bridge's slow vascular system of calcium, stone, and water. The cellular movements of a body, slowed ten-fold. Somewhere deep in the poured rock, a skeleton of twisted rebar.

2
Double arched, the masonry's Spartan, crumbling. Cracks are ubiquitous, reddish against grey, webbed like a gin-blossomed nose. During the freshet the first arch takes the creek's overflow; in late summer it spans black river mud and vetch. The bridge speaks in other voices, calls in car rumble and echo. The echoes are well-known. No need to yell. It'll take the lightest whisper, the shyest *hullo*, and bend it around itself, juggle it, channel it back and forth, play the air and its subtle compressions. Call out loudly—maybe your beloved's name—and you feel the echo palpitating your chest, searching out your hollows, your own bridge-like curves and arches.

3
The bridge is the inside of a mouth, a room of two windows. The bridge is liminal, unsure of its spatial status. Some days

container, shelter; some days opening, a conduit for the wind. The bridge looks best when reflecting the creek's currents—concrete taking the flux and curl of shallow pools, the liquid play of shadow on its blocky underside. When calling out, as one is wont to do under a bridge, those shadows seem of a piece with your echo—sound mirroring light, its throb and periodicity.

4

The bridge craves stones skipped swiftly. It's thought the most perfect stones are almost extinct—decades of family and visitors scouring the creek's few feet of pebbled shore, eyes downcast, beers forgotten, intent on a palm-sized chunk of granite to nock between the thumb and forefinger's rubbery web, to skip the calm waters and crack against the abutment, or go wide to clink the far bank's meshed rock. Before it's found and one marks its inevitable imperfections, before the moment you kneel and palm it, the mind goes platonic, idealizes the skipping stone, a perfect mathematical object riding this foam-flecked surface—higher form milled by current and chance. Look hard and a good one might turn up, banded by feldspar and stuck among chunks of lichened schist. Wedge it up from the muck bed, careful to leave its concave negative scrolled with earwigs. Stand on the farm's side, feel the bridge's curve unrolling over you, widening in perspective as it arches back down to the other side. Extend your arm, muscles tensed and tendons stretched—their own bridge to the next moment when you come in low, sidearm, almost parallel to the red water. Stay down, on the plane of the stone, watch its path—a slight bend like a blade of foxtail. Twenty degrees is the skipping stone's optimal angle to water. Eight skips. Or twelve: those last few a blur of sun-flash and droplet, the skips merging, the stone seeming to hover there on the surface, an oblong having little to do with water. Or maybe it rode the creek's lazy scrim in a Zeno's paradox of skips, each skip smaller by half, going and going but never reaching the other side.

Bull

1
The bull is never seen, but exists as possibility surrounding the alders. The bull is a *could*, a *perhaps* that haunts the field's outer copses. It is nowhere, so it is everywhere—a red-eyed potential stretched over wheatgrass and fern. When the cousins jump the electric fence to wander the field, the farm's neighbouring property, to kick at cow patties and catch bullfrogs, they are on the lookout—a charging cartoon, insane, nose-ringed, the worst bull because it is a bull made-up, rippled muscle and hoof smoke. The cousins only see cows crowding the field's one rock pond. The cows steer clear, placid Holsteins, boring, bored, moored, unmoved when the cousins machinegun crab apples at their flanks. The cousins enter the field tired of the farm's paths, hungry for borders. The bull is an outgrowth of their boredom, a dull afternoon's reverie. Desire in the head of a ten-year-old.

2
The bull's aura, its imagined presence, gives the field its worth, defines yellowed acreage. The cousins enter the field elated. The bull is a change in atmosphere, a charge, a tensile pleasure on the back of the neck, an emanation from the wooded fringes. It might enter. It might enter and they would have to run. Any minute now. If they know the word *gorge*, and some of them do, they see the bull—the word merging with the bull. Gorge *is* the bull. The bull is all around them, it is all direction. Without it, the cousins would

pass the field, wouldn't think to enter. They look over their shoulders while they walk the long grass, hoping to cure summer boredom while the adults, far away, know nothing of the bull. Later, tucked into the farm's upper rooms, they drift to guitar twang and laughter from the kitchen. Stretched headlights walk the floral wallpaper, flash in the amber eyes of their grandmother's doll collection. The bull was never there, never more present. In the minds of the sun-doped children, change is forever charging.

Canoe

1
To a Cooper's Hawk at cruise altitude, the canoe is Belleisle Creek's wound, its squinting eye with a crow's foot wake. Something cinched, ripping the morning's unruffled silk. The oars dimple the pool like the legs of striders ripping through their field of surface tension. Flipped among cattail and flattened lake stone, the canoe suns its epoxied hull, keel like a mule's protruding spine. The canoe is most stable while sated with ballast—innards stuffed with sloughed life jackets and cooler; but standing water and spilt beer slosh to the gunwales when drunks overstep while boarding. One should know the canoe is tetchy, not yet broke—shift your weight for that last Labatt's and she'll throw you. A canoe on her beam ends is the shore's toothless grin. A canoe is open at the top but its skeleton extends as thwarts, cross braces stretched gunnel to gunnel.

2
During mating season, the canoe intentionally gets stuck, catches up on rock. It finds eddies to spin in, and waits. Its notched fishing rod proboscis isn't for brook trout but other boats. They circle each other, tangled, attached by gossamer

thread. The canoe have no mouth, possess no larynx or syrinx; all ribcage, they use their bodies like cicadas. The canoe speak echoic monosyllables, reflecting the shallows, a voice of aqueous depth like stones rubbing underwater. To mimic the canoe's call, you need a wooden bucket and freshwater, you must think hollowness, pockets of air displacing bone and body fluids. You must learn the drippy phonetics of resonant things. The canoe's morphology hasn't changed for a hundred million years, a bilateral carapace like the inner segments of ancient arthropods. Some go back further, theorize that the canoe evolved from algal cells—a gigantic diatom cutting the water.

Creek

Often bastardized as crick. The creek stills for tubing, for summer canoes, but its heart pumps in spring, bringing the freshet's tonnage of broken ice. Uncles ride the floes, slipping up bergs without spilling rum and cokes. After bad winters, the spring ice leaves the farm's paths gutted, chunks the size of barbeques gouging out grass and earth—some morainal event in sped-up miniature.

The shadow of an inner tube slipping ripple-like over the creek's stony floor is darker than the tube's own sun-faded black, a black gone charcoal, almost white at the tube's stretched seams. While floating on the creek, the cousins might try to spear a trout with a five-inch galvanized nail duct taped to a sawed-off hockey stick, something your uncles made to keep you busy, out of the way; you might keep your child's frame taut above the tube, knees balanced on either side, the creek in its reflected light, its contained glare, like its own winding sun; and you might try to bring the tip to the water's surface, a slow approach before the plunge; you might see the trout still on the bottom, its shadow a sharp ellipsoid underneath it, more prominent than the fish, it's what you saw first, the fish almost camouflaged in creek light, everything the same shade a few feet down; and how proud you'd be to bring up this fish from the creek's bottom in a flash of spume and foam; but the creek won't let you get the fish, will allow you to waver, unsteady above its unmoving length; and when you bring the homemade spear down at what you think is the fish, a sure shot, it's gone in a puff of silt-smoke; and you see as you teeter—as you bring the spear up in an arc of river spray—that you weren't even close, that there was too much at play—angle and speed, refraction, shadow, the limbic fish mind all reflex, eons outside of calculation—and there will never be anything torqueing itself on the rusted end of your makeshift spear. So bring your tube towards shore, pull it along as you walk against the creek's weak but persistent current, your gait spacewalk slow. Drag it across the creek's short beach, pebbled river sand stuck to its underside. Pocket a stone whose patterned minerals played the light best. The creek will let you take this.

Deer

A family perhaps—whitetails yo-yoing across the back fields, out for choke cherries, crab apples fermenting in the dead grass. They move in a soundless gallop, no clop or hoofbeat; there's a lightness when they cross the field, as if showing deference to the ground. They eventually notice one of the cousins, and they stop when he moves, when he takes a sip from his coffee, alone, twenty feet above on the deck of the new place. Eight heads swiveled on slender necks—all tendon, jaw, and veined muzzle. Face-on they're trifoliate, ears and head leafy lobes radiating from the forehead's centre. The cousin stops mid-sip, coffee steam flexing into September's chill morning. Unmoving, cold, he takes in their canted attention, all heads oriented at the same angle. There's a consistency here, a pattern he could plot against the chaos of leaf, branch, weed, cloud, breeze. They pull the day out of its disorder and variegation. They make an arrangement, a structure. And he feels caught out, scrutinized, a trespasser on this abandoned acreage. He's enveloped in their dichromatic, UV glow. But he also feels a reciprocity, a brief sharing of the morning. He feels jittery but level, attentive, hyperaware of movement; he feels what he imagines to be deer-like. Then: a transfer. It's been too long. He has been greedy with stillness. Presumptuous. The balance teeters, collapses. One deer flicks an ear, there's a flinch of hocks and fetlock, an energy runnelling through the group, and one takes off in a jumping lope, and another one beside it—a partner perhaps—runs, too, towards the pines surrounding the fields. The cousin remains still but can't track them. Somehow, even watching, he misses where they go. He's lost the thread, their disparate directions. Not an exit so much as a dissipation. They leave like mist, like weather changing.

Dulse

Lobed like an oak with no midrib. Among the bladder wrack and sea lettuce, its quarter-machine sticky hands palm the Fundy's coastal sea rock. Dried out and packaged, slick transparency gone opaque and shrivelled, it's the farm's go-to snack, perpetually there among the dropped ash and empties. With the tide in, it waved its frill in the shallows. Now the cousins want chips, they want Heath bars, but they take a handful of *Palmaria palmata* from the crackling cellophane, chew and chew and taste nothing but fishy brine. Hours until supper; this is all there is.

Eel

They are engendered from mud and for this reason, if you catch hold of an eel, the creature is so slippery that the harder you press it the more quickly it slips away.

— T. H. White, *The Book of Beasts, Being a Translation from a Latin Bestiary of the Twelfth Century*

An anomaly among the day's full keel of trout. A writhing ouroboros wrapped tight to the line. But the eel on a hook was like any fish, stuck and bleeding, disfiguring itself on the tiny barb. It's caught during a trip with a local—one of the farm's many family friends. A red-faced man, slightly unhinged, he takes the cousins to his secret spot. To get there, they duck through corrugated sewer pipe long out of use, spider nests lining its roof like dome lights, come out at an enclosed water hole fed by one of the Belleisle's thin tributaries.

The eel needs unwinding, flat head buried inside itself, finally slackening as it dies. They impale it on a stick along with the fish—through the gills and out the mouth, a trick the man knew, a row of slick dead things hanging by their jaws. The eel swings from an alder branch, boneless and fully extended like the cousins' toy rubber snakes, one long fin ribboning its bottom half. The cousin who has caught the eel is slightly sickened, slightly proud. The eel is ancient, mud-born, pit-born, a single linear wave making its way up countless streams from its birthplace in the sea.

No one knows how to prepare it, so the cousin crosses the farm's road and tosses it in Belleisle Creek— silver and black helicoptering over the bank, catching the sun.

Elephant

This tusk is all that remains. Reminds. Although isolated reports state that mastodons were once native to the area, grazing shrubs during the late Pleistocene, this is definitively not a mastodon tusk. It's contemporary, yellow white, beside the TV in the farm's living room, and comes from a poached African elephant. A carved mask stretches its length from the mount. To the cousins, the living room is a kind of lazy wunderkammer, instilling boredom more than wonder, dusty and postcolonial, full of their grandfather's gifts from legislative world travels—hand-painted Matryoshka dolls, Inuit soapstone, decorative plates from Norway. And the tusk: the largest of the farm's knicknacks. The living room goes museum dark at the height of summer noons; the cousins pass through quickly en route to the barn or the kitchen or the screen door leading to the deck and the field and the field's branching paths. But sometimes, stuck inside, corralled before family dinners, the cousins run their fingers along the tusk's gouge and kerf, wondering if it's real. The cousins, on tiptoe, look down the tusk's hollowed interior, and they think of sanded wood or shells. It widens in the curve, for the top they look down is really the base, where the tusk was pried from the dying elephant's skull.

Fur Coat

It is said that fur coats feed on perfume spritzed from crystal atomizers and the smoke of thin menthols. It takes 20 fox, 60 mink to make one. The fur coats of the dead are doubly bereft, mourning the animals they once were and the spirits of their departed occupants. They are loose skins defined by lack. They are made from the dead but not quite dead themselves, held alive in the collective memory of past owners, of handed-down family members. The farm's fur coat is hibernating, sinking into its hanger in the hall closet of the new place. It waits for recently dead, encased in a zippered drycleaner's bag, wide cuffs flat to its sides. The fur coat remembers being helped from shoulders by maître d's, remembers Europe. Hangs onto nothing but its own trapped scent—the musk of Calvin Klein, old molecules held deep in the fur. Family enter the new place and they smell it still—a faint permeation, a whiff, a ghost.

Guitar

Baleen strings that sieved song, ate down picks piecemeal, triangular to blunt oval—the nub of a season. Spring sunburst, winter a seal-black coat. Turning in summer bonfires, the cousins catch a pulse of red before it retreats to the shadows— the dreadnought outline of topboard in pure reflected light, the sound hole a surprised mouth. Nervous, never lulled by blues-scale proficiency. Skittish with the fancy shit, it'll break its high E on a solo, split your pinkie like a lip. Most at home with its mouldy strings buzzing an off-key G-C-D, an uncle's loose-limbed and absent strum, it comes through doors eager, vibrating in its plush maroon interior. During lean months use a bread tag for feed, to make it sing.

Housefly

The average person probably has done more casual observing of houseflies than of any other insect. And yet, since flies in our houses are looked upon mostly with disgust, the observations were probably not terribly objective or scientific.

— Stokes Guide to Observing Insect Lives

They do not burst when stepped on but conform to heel pads like dropped raisins. Houseflies at the farm are a staple, their flight paths a necessary part of the kitchen's wild ecosystem of smoke and voice and movement. The flies land and uncles and aunts go swatting, swatting without stopping to slow the anecdote they were getting to the lurid end of. Come fall, window sills are a black wool of thorax and iridescent wing. The swatter is in the farm's pantry, a place of honor, the nail it hangs from made vague with coats of paint— more daub now than nail. The swatter is of the common species—porous plastic hand attached to lengths of braided metal. To kill a fly, there must be technique, a certain grace, an economy of movement. No wild swings; no mobster-with-a-bat aggression. The deft choses the wrist flick over the wide arc. Remember: flies are nerve incarnate, all reaction and heightened sense. They taste with their feet.

 Years later, a cousin will visit the property's new place (no longer new but always the new place). It will be inundated, a dustpan's-worth on the floor each week. When his grandparents built the new place they said that the draw was new wood—fresh pine's spice and gum, generations breeding in the walls. But they're still here, decades later, like a haunting. Before bed, without a swatter, the cousin will kill five swarming the ceiling fan's three splayed bulbs. Using a book, he'll swing and cuss, the cover's matte going greasy with the glaucous beads of their interiors. It isn't the buzzing that grates but the insistent knock of small bodies—a quiet ping on the lamps' frosted shades. And yet there's comfort in flies, for they are part of his youth, their small bodies and constant buzz always there during visits.

Icicle

If close enough, and at the right point in their life cycle, two icicles on the farm's back eave will begin a midwinter merger. The cousins note that, fused, the icicles become the barrels of their grandfather's over-and-under shotgun.

Inner Tube

1

Inner tubes are invertebrates only recently evolved for land. As sea creatures they floated in darkness, diaphanous, and fed on the dust of dead creatures from upper currents. The inner tubes of the farm are gorged on air and pumped to bouncing pressure. They nest in the chicken coop. The farm's inner tubes are most at home while being rolled down hills, while the cousins balance inside, grabbing long brass valves like rudimentary handles to some Victorian one-wheeled steam-powered wonder, going end over end until they spill out, momentum lost, the tube still rolling beyond them, settling like a spun coin oscillating on its edge.

2

Being inner, they're of the internal, the half-glimpsed—organ, wound. They were the oft-contained, the pressurized inner skin of an eighteen-wheeler, now set free to bloat, to spread their skin, to glut on air far from the truck tire's vulcanized prison. Some are emaciated and patched like old jeans, unable to keep their air, weak for bouncing. Some are thick and hale, trampoline-ready: the ones the cousins fight over. Some are segmented, cinched—infinite circular worms. Left out, they make yellow circles in the grass.

3

The inner tube is stackable, and the cousins create an upright tunnel to stand in. One stands in the centre of its centre, smelling crab grass and old rubber. From the outside the cousin is a floating head, a body articulated, centipedal. The tubes welcome the body heat, the breath and sweat and anticipatory fear. The others run and there's a bracing for impact, a hope each valve is aligned to avoid soft spots. The cousin is knocked on the grass, moving through their series of tubes, peristaltic. Hot, slightly panicked, and then they're out, hair mussed, red face upturned to the sky.

4
The inner tubes are no longer there. On a recent visit, a cousin, older now, hoped to find one dead and flattened, its valve pointing up and burnished from a loose skin of rubber. But the chicken coop was empty. Or they left, rolled away one autumn years after the farm closed up. They nudged the shed's overgrown door, still holding their decades-old air, bouncing through the fields and into the woods, finally free.

Leech

The cousins know the creek has leeches. It's infested—slick bodies curling in stagnant depths. After summer dips, the cousins surreptitiously check themselves over on the rocky sand; each piece of river dirt on pale skin makes them jump. Forgotten mole and freckle momentarily becomes leech. When the creek lowers in August, slow foam on the surface, the cousins are vigilant. Yet only one ever gets a leech. Panicky wheezing, clawing hands, the leech small and thin, a wet film on his hairless calf. Despite what they say they don't need to burn it off. And really it could have been a fleck of leaf. The creek may not have leeches. The creek is full of leeches.

Lightning Rods

Like the order *Hymenoptera*, there are thousands of species and subspecies, each distinguished by the glass ball at their iron rod's base, bulbous like an insect's abdomen. The farm's lightning rods aren't as elaborate as some antiques, for whose blown glass bulbs—scalloped and ribbed in colourful liquidity, vase-like—collectors pay a premium. The spheres on the farm's lightning rods are hardly decorative. They are not perfectly round but strombuliform—spinning tops. They don't share the glassine brightness of the more coveted shapes; their polished white is more like porcelain. No matter the rust and dun of the structures they protect, the bulbs seem unaffected by weather. The rods ride the arches of the roofs—the farm and its connected barn—part of their vascular systems, each rod connected to a frayed copper wire that snakes down the wall for grounding. Lightning strikes are a standard for measuring unlikelihood. The odds are the farm won't be struck. The odds are the farm won't last the decade. But the lightning rods wait, point to the clear sky, patient points of receptivity.

Minnow

The creek's anxious ticking and itch, its littoral pins-and-needles. Tiny slips of scale bobbing in the bathwater shallows, they flit in the shadows of rubber boots; lift a foot and silvered quickness punctuates the slow weave of a creek bed. The cousins net them—darker now against bucket-white. The minnows float at the sides, unmoving, compass needles pointing to some shifting magnetic north. They're poured into jam jars, the tiny kind from gift baskets, and left on the cobwebbed window ledge of the barn's loft. Out of moving water, the minnows go belly up and barely there, strings of organs through transparent skin, filtering the window's dusty light.

Moose

The Farm's Moose exists as the single exemplar of the species, like some zoological specimen preserved in the bowels of the Smithsonian. The Farm's Moose fits in the cousins' small hands. Along with the tin model John Deeres, it's one of the farm's only toys. Unclear if the cousins love the moose for its uniqueness, or this scarcity. After all, its limbs cannot articulate, eyes do not light up. There is no hatched rectangular door under its belly for the housing of batteries. The Farm's Moose has that greasy look of worn velvet, haunches shined by the body's oils like ancient totems. Glued black beads for eyes. It stood atop the front closet, beside the small box that held labelled keys—*Back Door, Front Foor, New Place, Hall, Barn*. The Farm's Moose may be hollow. It's plastic and might have a base.

Pickup

F-150, medium blue. Mid-eighties, year unknown. A gun rack in the cab's back window—three sets of curved steel hooks covered in grippable rubber. Its rear holds a white cap with slanted windows. Everything seems to cant on this truck, a boxy lean through the chassis, the square grill like a jutting forehead. The cousins are in back, roofed, the blown fibreglass of the cap like the inner stipple of an egg carton. Inside it's all creak and bump, rolling tools, the oldest cousins calling the raised seats of the wheel wells, the tint of the windows skewing the roadside's passing trees. The rest bump and jostle like unsecured cargo as the truck takes its hard turns down logging roads, to fishing holes and walking trails, to Hatfield Point, to stone wharves on the Belleisle, to unnamed lakeshores for the launching of canoes. Even in daylight, to be in the pickup's capped box is to be in perpetual dimness, the window's light not enough, like a summer day threatening storm, like late autumn afternoons. In the truck's bed the cousins learn their centres, how to steady their bodies without the help of seat belts or hand holds. To compensate for inertial forces. Carried so, they feel safe despite the bumpy ride, the geographical not-quite-knowing. Although many trucks came before, it is the ur-truck for the cousins, what they always think of when they think *truck*; when, years later, someone says *half-ton*. The cap is attached to the box with c-clamps, rarely removed—a seasonal moult; it's the truck's hermit crab home. With the cap off the truck looks thin, rickety, overexposed to the sun. The truck carries its cousins like young. It stops; the back opens—the cousins unloaded to their destination.

Raspberry

The canes edge the farm's back fields, grow up through the deck's boards, twined with cow fence and Virginia Creeper. The cousins remember the easy way they slipped off their receptacles, leaving an inner cone stamped with the negative of each drupelet. They're doll cups, tart thimbles; they hold summer's solar energies then release them on the tongue. Years later, you stand in a wedge of fridge light in the predawn suburbs. You take a handful from their plastic vented container—supermarket berries, bulbous things approaching strawberry size, shipped from the States, not enough and never as good. Still, you pop them in one at a time, and you're lit with creek smell, mown grass, forearms scraped from overgrown paths; taste-memory from the edgelands.

Sleep

The cousins fall into the mouths of sleep, blotted out. Sleep is a different species at the farm—quick-limbed, hungry, welcoming. The sleep with which they're familiar, the sleep of the suburbs, is timid, unsure. It is a sleep that can be tamed, kept at bay. The cousins are young and have played hard; sleep was far from their minds when they kung fued off the field's inner tubes, swam against the creek's current like spawning salmon, hacked at skunk cabbage with spruce limbs in the surrounding woods. But always sleep waits inside, nocturnal, curled with the dust and housefly deadfall in the sloped-ceiling bedrooms. Later—much later, it seems to them, a whole life—the cousins are tucked under frayed quilts, and by the time their parents retreat down the stairwell, they're already out. Sleep came quickly and gently. And the cousins experience a sleep so much deeper than what they've come to know, a newborn sleep. Sleep is aware now, awake, more than lucid. And if sleep should start, retreat, it will be that much more jarring when the cousins spring up to clutch at sheets, to listen. They'd swear something moved by the scrolled dresser. For now the cousins lay dreamless, while downstairs the party floats on like the hull of a canoe, well past midnight and so far above them.

Stove

Xylophagous—circular mouths gorging on crumbled newsprint, old lattice. Give it pulp, burl, heartwood; watch a scabrous sheaf of birch bark make a green-flamed fist. The stove's detachable coil handle hangs on a hook; its grooved end fits snug in the tiny notches on the burner's lids. This way, its mouths can open—a kind of jaw it keeps away from its body. When you slide open the lid with its handle, there's a fingernail paring of orange light, a thin moon of flickering. The stove exists in symbiosis with pans and kettles; they piggy-pack on the stove like oxpeckers on hippopotami, a shark's remora. The textured wrought-iron kettle has a coil handle, too, leading experts to believe they shared a common ancestor. The stove's chest opens onto the bright coals of cordwood. It carries a bonfire in its lungs, exhales upward. The farm's smell is part stove, always—not smoke but a foundational smell, the raw radiated heat of burnt wood settling underneath tobacco and must. Remembered heat still in the walls.

Virginia Creeper

Virginia Creeper takes over the now abandoned farm, palmate leaves obscuring white siding and four-pane country windows. Sharp boundaries blur, right angles rounded by foliage. The creeper challenges solidity—walls shimmering in the breeze. The farm's borders, then, are permeable; does its geometrical limits begin (or end) at its clapboard walls, or is the threshold found a foot out, at the leaves' jumbled reach? If one were to hide oneself among the brachiate bushwork of the creeper—face shadowed with leaf dapple, rural traffic dopplering beyond the spruce windbreak—would one be *within* the farm, looking out? Does the creeper extend the farm? Unknown if the creeper contributes to deteriorating structural integrity, if runners find holes in the brickwork, slip through gyprock and lathe. Roots crumbling the foundation. Maybe the opposite is true, and the creeper is necessary, woody tendrils holding up strut and crossbeam. Which is it—extra muscle or cancer? We do know that the farm is gift-wrapped, hog-tied, held in nature's impossible marine knots. Sheet bend. Clove hitch. Bowline. Cat's paw. The farm is more creeper now than wood, pipe, or shingle. Now hollow roomed, all mote and spoor and droppings, its vitality is exteriorized. An observer passing on the highway will note the creeper, not the farm itself. Or rather they think they will note the farm, but what they will really see, what will strike them first, is the creeper, a two-hundred-year-old structure's chlorophyll pelt. The leafy vines make a skin, a skein, a weave of vein pumping life through fractal ladders of fibrous cells. Or it's a net. Chains. When the farm's finally bulldozed, the creeper will hold to the broken bits like grasping hands. In winter the farm's walls are slashed with the creeper's naked branches, like the January sky is trying to scratch it all out.

Well

The farm's well is taboo, so the cousins love the well. Yet truly they don't love it so much as its cover—rounded barn board surface, red and cracked like the farm's front door. The well doesn't reach above ground like storybook wells, but is level with the yard, hard to see when the grass is up. The cover's slats attach to nothing but themselves, the earth scabbed over their edges. There is a fake well beside the real well—a lawn ornament, mere decoration, complete with hand crank not meant for cranking, a little gabled roof. Sometimes, bored, the cousins will crank the crank, try to imagine rescues, treasure, something slick and enchanted curled in the bottom of a galvanized bucket. But the real well, close by, invites, speaks of entrances—two isosceles hinges in the ground, riveted and medieval. While the fake well opens to grass, to nothing at all, the real one contains depths, hides them, an unplumbed cylinder of void. The older cousins dare each other to jump it, to speed-walk its cover. They do a bent-kneed jumpless bounce—that move fearless kids do on elevators. To stand upon it is to feel alive, outside the rule of adulthood; to feel give, weightlessness, to imagine falling. The cousins don't wish to see inside the well; it is much deeper unopened. Their well, conditional, is all throat, an endless body burrowed through clay, shale, groundwater. A rock from a clenched fist might fall forever.

THE BELLEISLE REMNANTS

> Those ghostly traces, photographs, supply the token presence of the dispersed relatives. A family's photograph album is generally about the extended family—and, often, is all that remains of it.
>
> — Susan Sontag, "In Plato's Cave"

Wall Socket Adapters

The first few things in the first few boxes. The smallest boxes because I am in over my head. I'm at the new place, a double garage carriage house built on my grandparent's property in the early nineties, extra space to party and host holiday dinners. I'm here to ostensibly go through Grampie's papers. I have sketchy plans to be methodical, diligent, but I call my wife in tears.

*

When the original farm house got too old and too small, we'd gather at the new place, put together a line of paint-flaked picnic tables and cover them in old cloths, the garage doors opened a crack to let out the cigarette smoke and pipe smoke and dope smoke and stove smoke, a family tree of smoke dissipating into darkening fall air because we were a family of smoke, bonfire-makers, packers of rollies and fruity pipe tobacco. Late summer and I've finally come to breathe in this mould, this smoke still in the beams. Grampie's decaying boxes languish here, with their accordion files of dictated letters and legislative memoranda. They haven't moved in decades and I am no archivist. Boxes flatten other boxes, all unlabelled. I assume Grampie airmailed them from Ottawa when he retired in the early nineties, a future project for some intrepid CBC journalist. I am standing here surrounded by the past, the only sound the houseflies knocking the garage's single naked blub, and I am not that journalist. I open a long banker's box and the mildewed files sag in the moisture like fish gills. The boxes lean against spiderwebbed windows, dozens of them among wood panelled walls full with calligraphic honours and framed political cartoons—Grampie giant-headed, the Merrithew pug nose exaggerated.

*

I am unequipped, cannot distill this man.

*

Inside the smallest box there are two smaller boxes still, and I wonder how deep the boxes will go, containers nesting within each other like Nanny's Matryoshka doll, the one I loved as a child because it kept going, the last doll so small it was unpainted, the size of a fennel seed. I flip the lid of a cigar box—*Tabac Havane*—full of lapel pins, Military ribbon bars, tie clips baring coats-of arms. I assume the silver railway spike is some honorary gift from CNR until I notice the *Labatt's* logo. I decide this is significant because the spike came with a case of beer, and cases of beer were undoubtedly everywhere at the farm during my childhood, the strong corrugated kind built like moving boxes. Grampie wasn't a beer drinker—he preferred gin with lime cordial, home batch merlot—but everyone else held beers loosely, uncles popped caps on their belt buckles, twisted them open on the skin of their bellies, and I'd sneak sips after playing in the fields. So the spike serves as a totally legitimate relic of my grandfather's history, as valuable as any other trinket.

I don't understand the next one—a shoebox whose objects make little sense. It's a Cornell Box of bakelite and raw brass, thrown among a moth eaten Officer Cadet's uniform: wall socket adapters, their tubular backsides in various configurations of voltage and current. They seem anomalous, out of context. But what exactly is the context here? I could've found anything, or nothing; I had no expectations. They seem like alien technologies dropped here in rural New Brunswick. None of the adapters are in duplicate, each pronged arrangement unique to its country. Grampie, ever diligent and organized, tucking the appropriate plug into the mesh pocket of his carry-on bag, these small tokens of well-heeled privilege. He plugs in his electric razor in a Helsinki highrise, in Osaka, in Paris, and feels the satisfaction of the right fit, the completed circuit, his three-piece ironed and waiting on the back of the suite's leather club chair.

*

Materiality, the unexpected detail of the diminutive: how I might find him, the version I can approach.

*

Grampie was a meticulous pack-rat; in the late seventies he bought an old community hall to store his shit, a church-like pile that rots on the property, storage for his grandkids. The adaptors, nested in their military uniform like electromechanical eggs, seem apropos of a man who kept everything. But I can't think of something less needed. Completely divorced from their utility, they represent a uselessness that aspires to its own art. Scattered throughout Canada, there is extended family for whom these adapters mean nothing. Do they mean any less than the other knickknacks? Dusty honours no one thought to keep. I'm cold and it's getting dark in this vacant museum. I don't take the adapters with me but later wish I had. I'd root through the box when I missed him, try to ground the circuit.

Lantern Flashlights

Yellow plastic and a 6-volt Rayovac, the battery's coiled ends sproinging when you unscrewed the flashlight's top like a jar of preserves. The funnelled reflective risk and the tiny teardrop bulb. Some nights Grampie took the grandkids for nature walks, jaunts where he'd ID his farm's flora and fauna in cooked-up Latin. We ran ahead, beams bouncing in time with our child's lope, lightsabers at the ready, dandelion heads knocking the tops of our rubber boots. The 6-volt's weight shifted like swung luggage in the casing. I pointed into night fog, cloud cover; bats sliced parabolas through the cone. The beam had a way of foreshortening the sky, making a backdrop of the firmament. I felt encased despite the distance: some ancestral belief of finitude. How quickly the light disappeared when I depressed the deep top button with my thumb. Instantaneous, gone in a click. So much height and reach, weightless kilometers.

*

Not quite weightless; I could swear the beam gave the flashlight heft, its extended substance something I could feel in the handle, pulling on my grip. Could I have remembered a slight curve to the light? The beam refracting through the atmosphere's particulate medium of water vapour and dust? Neck arched, I'd jump constellations—out of the cup of Ursa Major and into the wedged lap of Cassiopeia. Like you were holding a section of the Milky Way, quadrillions of photons travelling parsecs in a flick of the wrist.

*

GSM on three sides, always. Grampie was notorious for initialling his stuff, and permanent markers littered the farm. He had a brand—thick tubes armored in a metal case, the most permanent of permanent. My cousins and I took illicit sniffs for a cell-killing jolt. Nothing like the box of weak *Mr. Sketch* in Mrs. King's first grade classroom, each colour an underwhelming chemical stab at fruit, their tips mashed by the noses of kids desperate for candied molecules. Grampie used his markers to initial tools, key fobs, jacket tags, the inside sweat-dark leather of work boots. *GSM* on the container where he kept the pungent tangle of his pipe tobacco. *GSM* on the plastic mickey that held his gin, the bottle tucked safely inside the breast pocket of an army surplus jacket. Why so diligent? Such an overly proprietary gesture in Kings County. The farm often had guests, locals and friends of friends, pop-ins extending well beyond extended family. Was he wary of strangers? As a retired federal minister, he undoubtedly had trust issues.

The thieves, it turns out, were his own kids. My uncle tells me he still has Grampie's shovel, a pair of boots, and 9/16th inch socket wrench he never returned. *GSM* on it all. *I'm surprised he didn't get Nanny tattooed with it*, one aunt says. In my twenties I tattooed *GSM* along my right bicep with Grampie's birth and death dates on the inside of my elbow—what tattoo artists call *the ditch*. A different means of achieving permanence: *GSM* in tough guy Blackletter, the go-to typeface for text-based tattooing, pointy and lashed together like each grapheme was tricked out in bondage gear. Grampie would have called me a fool, a goof. But I own nothing with *GSM*.

*

The farm's been cleared out for years, his inscribed paraphernalia dispersed. But much of my childhood carries his signatory: the way he'd brush away leaf fall from a jack-in-the-pulpit, careful not to disturb its dipping purple leaf; puffing his pipe at the farm's head table in the front room, surveying a jumble of lit cigarette and passed plate, calling *Harken*, his go-to archaism to quiet the din, guffaws fading to small vitric clinks, tines on a wine glass; telling us the black knot fungi on the choke cherry bush were turds ejected from passing planes; the last time I saw him alive, wrapped in a blanket, his cheek stubble like bark on snow; and walking beside him, our flashlights ghosting the tree wall rounding the farm's back fields, pools of light rippling through the gaps. If those small eidetic bits—existing somewhere between photograph and recollection—could somehow obtain physicality, their backs would hold a blocky *GSM*.

*

He must've been okay with it, his things lost to the void on quiet Tuesdays after long weekends. Grampie signs his initials while grinning at a future disappearance: possible scenarios worked out and accounted for. Uncle Wayne stepping into his rubber boots, those heavy-duty models that tied at the top, the ones he always wanted, nice and high and camo green. A winter coat slipped on by a half-cousin during a bottle-strewn leave-taking. And now his sons and daughters rifle through tool boxes and closets long after he's gone, his markered name a reminder but also a wink, a subtle haunting.

*

At least one flashlight remains. I came upon it recently in the new place, the Rayovac still inside. His initials were there, too. Legible but faded.

Wineglass

The gazebo still holds his final drink. The day they took Grampie to the hospital, and he knew he wasn't coming back to the farm, he went out to sip homebrew merlot among his finch feeders and a rosebush so large it overtook half the front yard. Fifteen years ago and the wineglass is opaque with dust, the dew and weather of five thousand mornings. I'm staggered that it hasn't fallen over—the slow curved roll to the table ledge, the crystalline pop.

*

No one enters.

*

Last summer I was tempted, but entering seemed an imposition, a soiling of sacred ground. The gazebo was a shrine, a reliquary. The fact it's a wineglass—cup, grail—only contributes to Grampie's mythology. There's no official orthodoxy about disturbing the gazebo, but the wineglass is talismanic now, a charm against bad weather.

*

Octagonal, pre-fab, the gazebo edges a dip in the property, a small hillock that rolls down to Belleisle creek. One has a great view from here—the washed out wooded path my uncle kept up called *Wayne's Lane*; creek flash through the bulrushes. Inside, a single lawn chair and a round deck table. Leaf litter drifts through a crack in the door. Screen-filtered light hits the chair backing and invites one to take a seat. There might be a newspaper weathered to pulp. There might be the slightest tinge of pink still in the glass—the way empty reds, left out overnight, leave a flyspeck of sediment in the centre of the goblet's bowl. Less stain than change of light when you press your forehead to the screen for a closer look. Hard to say. Hard to say because screens have that way of destabilizing vision. Too close and your eye focuses on the screen itself, objects beyond merging to a blurred background against a plane of crossed wires. Or you focus past the screen, will it into invisibility, but the details—the glass, the chair—retain pixelated edges, caught in the screen's permeable weave. This is how memory works, how time might be an outdoor window screen you can't quite disregard; there's so much to see inside but that membrane will never allow for full resolution.

*

I won't enter.

*

My eye refocuses between screen and interior, a headachy dance. The pulled-out chair suggests return: gone but a minute, a top up. Or Nanny came to get him and they were rushed, *Let's go let's go*, interlocking arms as they made their way towards an idling car.

 They dined with royalty but Nanny drank rotgut scotch and Grampie's reds fermented in five gallon carboys. There was always wine in the new place, a small nook under the stairs Grampie called the wine cellar. Bottles breathing on picnic tables before Thanksgiving dinner. He is taking his last sip, twirling the wine and watching its legs. He thinks about tannins, acidity, the chemistry that brought him here. He thinks about the fecundity in which he's surrounded, the farm laced in Virginia Creeper, crabgrass breaking through the shifting plates of the driveway, fault lines that widen with each season. The spruce windbreak he planted against the highway, saplings dropped into their spaded plots: they're two stories tall now, boughs shadowing the front lawn. He thinks about how it will keep growing, the farm hidden from the road, reclaimed by surrounding vegetation. How things deteriorate but change into other things. Senescence and growth. He is getting up, hands locked to the chair arms. He takes his time, takes it in. It's late summer but he's draped in a hand-tied quilt. Normally he would bring his glass back in; he is fastidious that way. But right now it doesn't seem to matter. He wants his pipe. There's a finch.

Carousel Slide Projector

When we were kids Dad had a boxy Kodak that was all whirr and wind, a humming metabolism. It came with a screen that retracted with a zippered shush into an orange metal tube. Slideshows were saved for the farm—my relatives huddled on couches, watching slides curated from thousands Dad stored in plastic cases and kept in canvas duffel bags. I loved the dusty cone of light and that second of blackness before the next shot, the chunky click as each slide jumped into the bulb's glow. Some *ooh*-ed and *aah*-ed over, some tsked. Some quickly skipped with an awkward *awww*—an ex, a family friend on the outs.

Some farm memories, those of which I'm sure are slides: uncle Wayne popping a wheelie on a Honda trike; a life-size cutout of Grampie at a fishing trip, a cardboard simulacrum posed by uncles and friends at the stove, with a rod, waving to the camera with a wilted hunter's glove; my cousins and I, only months apart, sleeping in a row, and our sleepers match our baby chairs: blue, yellow, pink; a series from a rafting trip: flashes of life-vest and paddle through river spray; my uncle Gil massive in a small suit, demon-like with redeye; a foot long trout I caught with Grampie, the vague arch of it under ice in the farm's freezer; overexposed kitchen scenes: smokers and drinkers irradiated, as if the sun came inside.

*

All slides? Am I sure?

*

Wild raspberry overtakes the deck of the farm. Each board is secondary, structural support for hardy weed and roadside flora. Bushes and shrubs push through the interstices of spaced two-by-four and at one corner a small maple grows past the farm's lower roof—years ago a single samsara bearing its seed slipped through the deck's cracks, found a small edge with just enough sunlight to make a go of it. The entire thing a reclamation: coral taking over a sunken ship. The deck my aunts used to tan on, where my grandparents set out garden cukes and radishes in bowls of ice and vinegar, where my uncles rolled cigarettes and ate Fundy dulse from cellophane bags.

*

There's camcorder footage of a talent show on this deck. Early nineties. Wind-muted, the tracking off. We have a copy somewhere in my parents' basement, tucked in its white Fujifilm sleeve. I do a knock-knock joke that Grampie taught me, the same I told my grade one teacher on the first day of school. *Eileen who? Eileen over and you kiss my ass.* My older brother markers eyes and a nose on his chin and sings "Don't Worry Be Happy" upside down, his head hanging off one of the deck's wooden loungers, a small cardboard tuxedo taped to his forehead. My cousin does a magic trick; I remember a cigarette butt taped to the back of his thumb. We're seven or eight and terrible and our aunts and uncles are drunk and liking it all very much.

Was I nervous to tell my joke? Did I even tell the Eileen joke? Sparse specifics from Talent Show Day. I would have to watch the footage again, squinting through motion blur for the details. So many of our memories are magnetic tape, Kodachrome or pixel. There must've been a few years when the talent show footage and my memory of it existed in my mind simultaneously, a superposition of actualities. But they merged long ago, with a resultant filmic usurpation. I'm certain that what I call up now is the video footage. Or, rather, my memory of the footage, a thirdhand removal— not original memory, not the footage, but the footage sieved through subjectivity. Memory, always shaky, becomes drunk-on-a-balance-beam tottery. My squinting cousin showing a bent cigarette to a confused audience. Abracadabra.

*

The farm's front door is a cracked and scaly red, dermatitic, but its top window looks strangely clean, four fanned panes in a half-circle, reflecting ivy cover like still ponds. The handle's brass has gone dull, its hexagonal thumb press microns thinner from that small specific pressure: shoulder in, a downward push. My child's hands barely managed it. I preferred other entrances—the huge barn doors flimsy with age, the back deck's French doors.

You enter on a single doorstep, a 2 by 8 rounded to driftwood by the scuffing of ten thousand guests. Once painted black like the frame, now it's bone wood, each knot protruding like knuckles in an aging hand. Slight depressions from right and left feet.

There's a door knocker, too—a cardinal that pecked the wood when you yanked a string from its base. It's screwed to the farm's clapboard and no longer functional. The woodwork is competent but the paint has bled from its crest, exposing the grey wood's deepened grain.

I get an anxious twinge after studying the photos I took this summer: I'm not so sure this is the door knocker of my childhood. For one, it has no string. But it's more than that: something about the craftsmanship—the curved heft of it, hand-carved; a worked smoothness. It seems older, antique. The bird of my childhood was thinner, had less dimension— machine cut and gift shop chintzy.

I remember colours beyond a faded red.

More likely I'm mistaken: both birds are one and the same, and time has conferred some sheen of authenticity to it. Yet I remember the rough cut of the old bird's sides. I can't shake the difference. No matter: soon, this digital photo will be all there is.

*

Dad gets a slideshow ready. He holds the 35 mm wafers up to the light, and their inverted and oily surfaces materialize into clowning uncles, family portraits, dinner scenes with their doubled rows of tilting heads. Only the best are selected for that night's carousel—a ridged torus like a fossilized ammonite. My brother and I wrestle into the minivan with our Gameboys; we're headed to the farm for the weekend. Us kids will play the fool during the slideshow, mooning in front of the light. In the darkness of the farm's living room, staring down the projector, we become palimpsests, the photos stretching over us, taking on our dimensions while leaching us of colour. Each slide is slotted upside down and backwards—the projector's mirrors and convex lenses will right them. The same thing our brains do when we see.

NOTES AND SOURCES

On Halls, or, An Ashlar Falls to the Centre of the Earth

Benjamin, Abraham. "Understanding Our Membership Problems. *The Masonic Trowel*, www.themasonictrowel.com/leadership/management/membership_files/understanding_our_membership_problems.hm.

Hall, Manly P. *The Lost Keys of Freemasonry*. Macoy Publishing and Masonic Supply Company, Inc., 1976.

Macoy Rings Aprons Books – 10,000+ items for Freemasons. Macoy Publishing and Masonic Supply Co., www.macoy.com.

"Membership Totals since 1924." Masonic Service Association of North America, www.msana.com/msastats.asp#totals.

Ostendorff, Jon. "Masons, other service groups fight membership declines." USA Today, 31 Jan. 2011, usatoday30.usatoday.com/news/nation/2011-01-31-masons31_ST_N.htm.

"Rough and Perfect Ashlar." Masonic Lodge of Education, www.masonic-lodge-of-education.com/rough-and-perfect-ashlar.html.

The Weekend God: Alden Nowlan and the Poetry Weekend Fragments

Alden Nowlan: The Mysterious Naked Man. Directed by Brian Guns, National Film Board of Canada, 2004. Vimeo, uploaded by Brian Guns, 14 June 2017, vimeo.com/221605637.

Bartlett, Brian. "Nights in Windsor Castle: Remembering Alden Nowlan." *All Manner of Tackle: Living with Poetry,* Palimpsest Press, 2017, pp. 99-107.

Compton, Anne, Laurence Hutchman, Ross Leckie, and Robin McGrath, editors. *Coastlines.* Goose Lane Editions, 2002.

Dyer, Geoff. "A Note on Photographs." *But Beautiful: A Book About Jazz.* North Point Press, 1996, pp. ix-x.

Easy Reading for Adults. *Alden Nowlan: Writer and Poet.* Literacy Council of Fredericton, 1984.

Houle, Jennifer. *The Back Channels.* Signature Editions, 2016.

Keith, W. J. *Charles G. D. Roberts.* Copp Clark Publishing Co., 1969.

Leroux, John. *Building a University: The Architecture of UNB.* Goose Lane Editions, 2010.

Neilson, Shane. "This Charming Man." *Canadian Notes & Queries,* no. 92, 2015, pp. 52-55.

Nowlan, Alden. "About Memorials." *The Fiddlehead,* no. 137, 1983, pp. 21-29.

---. *Collected Poems*. Edited by Brian Bartlett, Goose Lane Editions, 2017.

---. *Selected Poems*. Edited by Patrick Lane and Lorna Crozier, Anansi, 1996.

Prouty, William. "Atlantic Soundings, New Brunswick." *The Fiddlehead*, no. 137, 1983, pp. 104-106.

Toner, Patrick. *If I Could Turn and Meet Myself: The Life of Alden Nowlan*. Goose Lane Editions, 2000.

Tinderbox: Dispatches from the Village of Fire

I owe a debt to the Petitcodiac Public Library's local archives. Without that ragtag collection of photographs, newspapers clippings, and village ephemera, I wouldn't have been able to write this piece. Some citations are spotty due to source condition and remaining information.

3 Black and white photos of the aftermath of a large fire. Date unknown. 4d, Box 1. Petitcodiac Public Library Archives.

Burrows, John. *Petitcodiac: A Village History*. New Brunswick Bicentennial Commission, 1984.

Graham, David. A. "Frozen Train Tracks? Set 'Em on Fire." The Atlantic, 1 Feb. 2019. www.theatlantic.com/technology/archive/2019/02/chicago-railroads-fire-tracks/581875/

Hibbert, Robert and Mary Hibbert. *Village of Fire*. R & M Printing and Publishing, 1996.

Morrison, Campbell. "Stroke of luck alerted family to major fire." *The Times-Transcript* (Moncton, NB), 21 August 1986, p. A1.

Nelson, Charlene. "Petitcodiac fire sweeps Main Street." Publication unknown. Date unknown.

Petitcodiac Village Council. *Village of Petitcodiac.* Tribune Press, 1969.

Pyne, Stephen J. *Fire: A Brief History.* University of Washington Press, 2001.

Rogers, Louise A. *Generational Memories: Life in the Village of Petitcodiac.* Louise A. Rogers, 2008.

Scrapbook of newspaper obituaries. Various dates. 2a, Box 2. Petitcodiac Public Library Archives.

Times-Transcript staff. "Charges slated in Petitcodiac fire." *The Times-Transcript,* date unknown (1993).

Times-Transcript staff. "Spectacular $2-M fire hits downtown Petitcodiac: Four firms are wiped out." *The Times-Transcript* (Moncton, NB), 20 August 1986, p. A1.

ACKNOWLEDGEMENTS

I gratefully acknowledge the support of ArtsNB, who provided funding during the writing of this project.

Deepest gratitude to the editors of the magazines in which some of these pieces previously appeared: *Grain, Hamilton Arts & Letters, The Malahat Review, Partisan,* and *PRISM International*. "Ghostly Transmissions from John D. Rockefeller" won First Prize in *PRISM International*'s 2015 Creative Nonfiction Contest. "Rooms" was shortlisted for the *Malahat Review*'s 2018 Constance Rooke Creative Nonfiction Prize. "A Field Guide to Northeastern Bonfires" originally appeared as a chapbook with Frog Hollow Press.

A huge thank you to my editor Shane Neilson: your tirelessness, availability, and enthusiasm got me through. You are a dynamo. Thanks to those who read parts of this book and helped me along the way, notably Allan Cooper, Dan Renton, and Jesse Jacobs. Endless love and respect to my parents, as well as my aunts and uncles, who patiently answered my questions about farm lore. Thank you to Chuck for giving me your blessing to write about your experience; you are one of the kindest and bravest men I know. Sarah and Molly: you give me so much, and this book wouldn't have happened without your constant love and encouragement. Every word is for both of you, because of both of you.

ABOUT THE AUTHOR

Danny Jacobs' poems, reviews, and essays have been published in a variety of journals across Canada, including *The Malahat Review*, *The Fiddlehead*, *Grain*, *The Walrus*, *Maisonneuve*, *PRISM International*, *Hazlitt*, and *Hamilton Arts & Letters*, among others. Danny won *PRISM International*'s 2015 Creative Nonfiction Contest and *The Malahat Review*'s 2016 P. K. Page Founders' Award. His first book, *Songs That Remind Us of Factories* (Nightwood, 2013), was shortlisted for the 2014 Acorn-Plantos Award for People's Poetry.

His poetry chapbook, *Loid*, came out with Frog Hollow Press in 2016. His latest work, *A Field Guide to Northeastern Bonfires*, is a hybrid lyrical essay/prose poem sequence published in 2018 with Frog Hollow's NB Chapbook Series.

Danny lives with his wife and daughter in Riverview, NB, and works as the librarian in the village of Petitcodiac.